Silhouette

A Play

Simon Brett

A Samuel French Acting Edition

SAMUEL FRENCH

FOUNDED 1830

SAMUELFRENCH-LONDON.CO.UK
SAMUELFRENCH.COM

FOR AMATEUR PRODUCTION ENQUIRIES

UNITED KINGDOM AND WORLD
EXCLUDING NORTH AMERICA
plays@SamuelFrench-London.co.uk
020 7255 4302/01

Each title is subject to availability from Samuel French,

depending upon country of performance.

SILHOUETTE

First presented at the Yvonne Arnaud Theatre, Guildford,
on 19th August, 1997 with the following cast:

Martin Powell	Jeremy Clyde
Detective Inspector Bruton	Joe McGann
Celia Wallis	Stephanie Beacham
Detective Sergeant Fisher	Craig Purnell
WPC Leach	Verity Anne Meldrum
Detective Constable Wilkins	Martin Belville
WPC Carter	Rachel Paris
Neville Smallwood	Hugh Dennis

Director Keith Baxter
Designer Simon Higlett
Lighting Vince Herbert

CHARACTERS

Martin Powell
Detective Inspector Bruton
Celia Wallis
Detective Sergeant Fisher
WPC Leach
Detective Constable Wilkins
WPC Carter
Neville Smallwood

The action takes place in Martin Powell's and Celia Wallis' country home in West Sussex. A Friday night in October

ACT I   About 9.15 p.m.
ACT II   7.30 p.m., *earlier* the same evening

AUTHOR'S NOTE

This is just a note to say: don't be daunted by the apparent scale of the play. It will still work on a much less grand scale than in its original production. On the professional stage we had the benefit of Simon Higlett's wonderful two-storey barn conversion, but *Silhouette* can also be performed, with the minimum of line changes, in a set representing a one-level country cottage with a door leading off to the bedrooms.

There can also be economies of cast. As printed here, it is a play with eight characters (5M 3F), but it could easily be done with six (4M 2F). The lines of Wilkins and Carter could be redistributed to Fisher and Leach. But if you can stretch to eight, it does help the play in two ways. First, in Act I it makes the stage look busy, and gives the impression of the Scene of Crime team taking over the house. Second – very important in a whodunit – it gives a wider range of potential murderers.

Silhouette requires a few special effects, but nothing beyond the skills of an inventive backstage team. The most important is, as the title might suggest, the silhouette, which is seen at various times behind the frosted panel of the front door. After experimenting with various methods of achieving this effect in the original production, we ended up using an old-fashioned piece of gauze attached on the back of the glass panel. With proper back-lighting of whoever – or whatever – was standing in the doorway, and with the onstage lights doused, this produced a very convincing and menacing outline.

A warning on sight-lines, which will I'm sure be obvious to any designer reading the play. The front door must be visible at all times from all parts of the auditorium. So must the chair in the study, where Martin's body is found (except of course when the study curtains are closed).

The shooting of Martin Powell's "Golden Heart" award in Act II is an intriguing challenge for any Stage Manager. We created the illusion by using a thin plaster heart painted gold, which was smashed by the release from offstage of a kind of sprung hammer behind it. This was of course timed to coincide with Neville's pulling the trigger and firing the rifle. But I'm sure there are other ways the effect could be achieved. (However you do it, you're going to need a good supply of Golden Hearts!)

The bloody appearance of Martin's body throughout Act I was created by using a detachable wound stuck to his face and a blood-soaked shirt identical with the clean shirt he wears for most of his time onstage in Act II. He has to revert to corpse mode for the end of Act II, but there is plenty of time for him to make that change. (Ideally, the "body" should be *in situ* right through Act I. If the actor playing Martin really can't face staying there that long, then at the times when the corpse is covered with a cloth, a dummy can be used.)

And, of course, for the back wall of the study you need two removable panels, a clean one for most of Act II, and a blood-spattered one for Act I and the very end of the play.

The final special effect, which provides the play's pay-off, is the blinking light from the cassette recorder right at the end. We did have an operational blinking light on the actual machine, but this couldn't be seen by many of the audience. After trying various effects, we found the one which made the point clearest was using a very thin focused beam of red light from directly above the table on which the cassette recorder was placed. As the main stage lights went down after Celia's final exit, this light built up and started to pulse, cross-fading with the rest of the stage lights going down to black. Then the curtain fell.

A point for directors of *Silhouette*. Because of the play's structure, with the events of Act II taking place chronologically before those of Act I, until the last week Keith Baxter, our director, rehearsed the play out of sequence. Rehearsing Act II before Act I does help the actors see the overall line of their characters' actions, as well as simplifying continuity for props, etc. Then, in the final week, when the performances were more or less set, we reversed the order of the Acts, and rehearsed the play as it would be presented in front of an audience. (This is not a *diktat* to directors. It's just a suggestion which might help. If it doesn't, ignore it.)

Finally, one note for the actors. In all stage thrillers, the audience is out there, trying to second-guess you. They're looking for clues, they're looking for inconsistencies in what you say and do. So you must play them at their own game. Act with truth, of course, but also act with a kind of playfulness. The central couple in *Silhouette* are both actors. Other characters may not be what they appear. Anyone might be lying at any moment. If the audience gets that feeling from the way you play the lines, they will enjoy themselves. And, hopefully, so will you.

Simon Brett

Other plays by Simon Brett
published by Samuel French Ltd

Mr Quigley's Revenge
Murder in Play
The Tale of Little Red Riding Hood — An Untraditional Pantomime

ACT I

The sitting-room and study of the country home of the actors Martin Powell and Celia Wallis. A Friday night in early October. About 9.15

The house is an expensively converted Sussex barn. The sitting-room is by far the biggest part of the set. There are three entrances to this room. UC, double doors open into Martin's study, a small room dominated by his large desk, on which is a desk lamp; there are pictures on the back wall. French windows open off the side of the study to the front garden. Either side of the double doors into the sitting-room are glass panels, over which curtains can be drawn. When these curtains and the doors are open and when there is sufficient light the audience can see everything in the study. The other sitting-room entrances are the door to the kitchen and the front door. The top half of the latter, which is in a recess, has a frosted glass panel. When backlit, the silhouette of anyone standing on the doorstep can be seen through the panel; when the sitting-room lights are on, nothing can be seen through the glass. There is a row of pegs for coats in the recess; on these hang an opera cloak, an expensive man's raincoat and two flamboyant wide-brimmed men's hats. Beneath the pegs is a long cricket bag. A staircase leads up to the first floor landing, off which a passage leads to a bathroom and Martin and Celia's bedrooms (though the doors to these are unseen). There is also a fireplace with a mantelpiece over it

The sitting-room contains a sofa and the usual complement of armchairs, coffee and occasional tables, drinks cupboard and drinks table (with a letter on it as well as all the drinks paraphernalia), as well as another desk (with papers, an address book and a large labelled Jiffy bag on it), a vase, telephone and a stereo unit. But what makes the biggest impression is the collection of theatrical memorabilia. Displayed on a life-size dummy is the complete costume worn by Martin Powell in "Henry VIII." There are framed posters and production photographs (including one of Martin Powell as Richard III), as well as citations and awards set in purpose-built niches. There is also a display of stage weaponry: guns, swords, daggers and so on. One of the mountings, where a rifle and ammunition belt are usually displayed, is empty (though a sheathed knife is still in position). The niche that should contain Martin Powell's "Variety Club Award for Best Actor in a Revival" contains not an award but a vase of flowers. The room is a shrine to the ego of Martin Powell (with a few nods towards his wife)

On the coffee table in front of the sofa is an empty champagne bottle. On a small table beside an armchair is a cassette recorder, covered with some pages of notes. An empty champagne flute stands on a shelf

The CURTAIN *rises. The stage is in near-total darkness; it is an almost moonless night. (Even this small amount of light beyond the windows fades to black as the play progresses.) Shapes, like the Henry VIII dummy, loom menacingly in the gloom. Eerie, dramatic music is being played at very loud volume on the stereo. The cassette recorder is on, with its small red recording light blinking*

In the study, Martin Powell, a striking-looking man some ten years older than his wife Celia, is slumped back in the chair behind his desk. He is dead, shot by a rifle bullet through the forehead. Blood has spilled down his face and on to his chest. Blood is spattered over the picture-covered wall behind him

There is the sound of a car approaching the front of the house. The noise of its tyres on the gravel of the drive is heard. The beam of the car's headlights sweeps across the stage, through the frosted glass of the front door and the french windows to Martin's study. This first sweep of lights is very brief, just giving a tantalizing snapshot of the scene inside the study. The hideous image is only glimpsed for a moment as the headlights sweep past, before they are switched off when the car is parked

The sound of a second approaching car on the gravel drive is heard. This one is a police panda. The beam of its headlights and the flickering blue of its overhead emergency flashers are projected on to the stage. The headlights sweep across the stage, slightly more slowly than the first car's, giving the audience a longer opportunity to see Martin's dead body. Then those headlights too are doused, but the blue lights continue to flash, intermittently illuminating the murder scene, until indicated

Detective Inspector Bruton approaches the front door, carrying a torch; the torchlight outlines his figure through the frosted glass panel. Detective Sergeant Fisher and WPC Leach are behind him. Bruton stops on the doorstep; his silhouette appears in the panel. He hammers on the door with his fist

Bruton Miss Wallis! Miss Wallis! It's the police!
Fisher Miss Wallis!
Bruton The front door's open. Miss Wallis!

Not waiting for a response, Bruton opens the unlocked front door and enters the sitting-room. He is about thirty-five and good-looking. For the first part of the act, Bruton is very much the traditional Police Inspector, dour, humourless, even a bit slow. Later in the act he becomes more menacing. Bruton is followed in by Fisher, a burly and taciturn plain-clothes man, and Leach, who wears uniform

Fisher closes the front door. There is now very little light, except from the torches and what spills through from the blue flashers in the drive. All three move into the room. Fisher bangs into something

Bruton (*irritated*) Fisher!
Fisher Sorry, sir.
Leach Where's that music coming from?
Fisher (*finding the stereo with his torch beam*) There's a stereo over here.

Bruton spreads the beam of his torch across the memorabilia-covered walls, lingering on the display of weaponry. Leach bumps into the Henry VIII dummy

Leach Aagh!

Fisher's torch picks out the Henry VIII dummy

Bruton Calm down, Leach.
Leach This place is like a museum.
Bruton No, Leach. It's just a house — (*with some contempt*) —where actors live. (*He calls out*) Miss Wallis! Miss Wallis!

There is no response

What were her exact words on the phone, Fisher?
Fisher (*shining his torch beam around the study*) "My husband's been murdered!" She kept saying, "My husband's been murdered!" (*His torch beam finds Martin's body*)

By chance, the music happens to hit an especially dark chord. At the sight of the blood-spattered body, Leach lets out a gasp that is almost a scream

Celia Wallis appears on the landing upstairs, looking very beautiful and very pale. She is an elegantly dressed, successful and attractive actress in her early forties. Normally she is full of vitality, funny and flirtatious, but at this moment she behaves exactly like a woman who has just discovered the body of her murdered husband

Bruton Well, she wasn't making it up, was she?
Celia No.

Bruton swings his torch beam upwards at the sound of Celia's voice

No, I wasn't making it up. It's real. (*She crosses to the landing light switch*)
We do have lights, you know. (*She switches on the landing light*)
Downstairs switches are on the beam.
Bruton (*getting out a mobile phone and dialling a number*) Fisher. And you
can turn that bloody music off too.

During the following, Fisher switches on the downstairs lights and stops the
music. It is suddenly very silent

(*Into the phone*) Wilkins, it's a murder all right. We're going to need the
Socko team. ... Exton's Barn, yes. (*He looks up at Celia*) I was calling you,
Miss Wallis. Didn't you hear me?
Celia (*coming down the stairs*) I'm sorry. I was in the bathroom ... trying
to pull myself together.
Bruton I'm sure you were. You don't remember me, Miss Wallis...
Celia (*stopping to look at Bruton properly for the first time*) Inspector
Bruton? From the Met? What are you doing in Sussex?
Bruton Transferred.
Celia Still in the Stalking Unit? (*During the following she comes fully*
downstairs and catches a glimpse of the scene in the study)
Bruton (*shaking his head*) Serious Crimes now. That includes murder.
Celia Moving from the terrified to the dead. Is that reckoned to be
promotion?
Bruton (*ignoring this*) And you remember Sergeant Fisher?
Fisher Good-evening, miss.
Bruton Fisher's a great fan of your work. Isn't that right, Fisher?
Fisher (*embarrassed*) Erm — Yes.
Bruton Television work, that is. Not theatre. Fisher's just your ordinary
average sort of person. So he doesn't go to the theatre. (*He indicates Leach*)
And this is WPC ——
Celia (*turning away from the study, very emotional*) No! I can't look at him!
Bruton Leach!

Leach comes forward quickly and leads Celia to sit down

(*Moving forward to the sofa*) This is WPC Leach, Miss Wallis. She's
trained in counselling, if you ——
Celia Oh, God, counselling! You can't do anything these days without being

counselled after it. They even have counsellors for people who've won the Lottery.

Bruton Wouldn't you say there was a difference between winning the Lottery and losing your husband?

Celia I'd say that depends on the husband.

Bruton Ah. (*He gestures to Leach to move away*)

Leach does as indicated

You're sure you're all right. Miss Wallis?

Celia (*with a great effort of will*) I'm in control. I'll be all right.

Bruton Good. I must just check out the crime scene, so if you'd like to keep facing that way … ?

Celia (*looking resolutely out front*) Thank you.

During the following we hear the sound of car tyres on gravel as the Scene of Crime Team's vehicles arrive. Bruton moves towards the study, putting on rubber gloves from his pocket. Fisher puts on rubber gloves too. Leach watches Celia with considerable intensity

Bruton Fisher.

Fisher moves towards the study. Martin's body is still intermittently illuminated by flashes of blue light. Bruton moves into the study, switches on the desk lamp, and looks at the body

Detective Constable Wilkins enters

Wilkins Inspector Bruton.

Bruton Ah, Wilkins! Be simpler if you bring the team in through here and get started.

Wilkins exits

You go and give them a hand, Fisher.

Fisher Sir.

Bruton Bring them back through the garden.

Fisher Very good, sir. (*He moves to the front door*)

Bruton And get them to turn off the flashers.

Fisher Sir.

Fisher goes out through the front door, and closes it behind him

Bruton crosses to look at the champagne flute on a shelf. The blue lights from outside stop flashing

Fisher enters through the french windows, carrying a couple of instrument cases, followed by Wilkins and WPC Carter. During the following they set to work in the study, setting up spotlights and investigating the body and the room

Bruton returns to the sitting-room and removes his rubber gloves. The curtains are drawn behind him

Bruton The Scene of Crime team'll take over now.
Celia Ah.
Bruton They'll start with the Police Surgeon confirming that your husband's dead..

Celia shudders

Leach will be here all the time I'm talking to you, Miss Wallis.
Celia Why?
Bruton Just so's we have a witness. So that we all agree on what's actually said.
Leach Do you want me to take notes, sir?
Bruton Thank you, Leach.
Celia Look, what is this? Am I under arrest?
Bruton No, of course not, Miss Wallis. It's just that when a male officer is questioning a female witness, it's often advisable to have someone else present.
Celia *(flirtatiously)* Are you afraid you might not be able to control yourself alone with me?
Bruton *(flatly)* I have no worries on that score.
Celia Thank you. I gather compliments weren't part of the Police College curriculum.
Bruton No. Well, it's certainly not a suicide.
Celia What makes you so sure?
Bruton No weapon. *(He indicates the weaponry on the walls)* Not, it seems, that you lack for weapons in this house, Miss Wallis.
Celia They're props. We used them in plays. *(She gestures to the wall)* Martin's *Tamburlaine* scimitar. My *Annie Get Your Gun* knife. His "pound of flesh" dagger.
Bruton What?
Leach For when he played Shylock, sir. In *The Merchant of Venice* at Stratford.

Bruton (*taking the* Annie Get Your Gun *knife — a small sheath knife — down and removing it from its sheath*) Ah.

Celia They're not real. The guns don't fire, the knives are blunted.

Bruton (*feeling the blade*) Seems sharp enough to me. (*He points to the Henry VIII dummy*) And who's this gentleman?

Celia Henry VIII. It's the costume my husband wore in another of his greatest roles.

Bruton (*trying to make a joke*) But he just had the one wife, did he?

Celia (*frostily*) I was his second.

Bruton (*moving on to change the subject*) Seem to be rather more mementoes from your husband's career than your own, Miss Wallis.

Celia That's the kind of actor Martin was. The kind who'd swim round and round a lighthouse to keep in the light.

Bruton Lighthouse? Didn't our Stalker write something about lighthouses? About you being the lighthouse of his life?

Celia The "lodestone" of his life. He said I was "the lodestone of his life."

Bruton Sick, some of the stuff he wrote in those letters, wasn't it? Still, at least he stopped six months ago, didn't he?

Celia Yes … (*She hesitates*) That is …

Bruton (*sharply*) Are you saying you've had some more?

Celia There was one. This week.

Bruton Do you still have it?

Celia (*nodding*) Yes. (*She gets the letter from the drinks table and brings it to Bruton*)

Bruton (*taking the letter and opening it*) Still typewritten. And his style doesn't change, does it? (*He reads*) "You will be mine. When you are on your own, I will come to you. And when our blood commingles, you will be mine forever. When my knife traces the soft contours of your skin, I'll ——"

Celia (*with a shudder*) Stop it.

Bruton Funny, isn't it? After a letter like that, you'd think I'd been called out here to investigate your murder, not your husband's.

Celia Yes. (*She realizes the full impact of what he's saying; with horror*) Yes … Oh God, I've just thought — I am on my own.

Bruton Sorry?

Celia Martin's dead. I'm on my own. The letter said that, when I'm on my own, he will come to me.

Bruton Yes. (*Brusquely*) However, the fact remains that you haven't been murdered, and your husband has. And that's the case I'm investigating.

Carter (*appearing through the curtains from the study*) Sir.

Bruton Yes, Carter?

Carter A single bullet fired from a rifle. At close range in the study.

Bruton Thank you.

Carter disappears back into the study

(*Getting a notebook out of his pocket*) When did you find your husband's
body, Miss Wallis?

Celia Only minutes before I phoned the police.

Bruton (*consulting the notebook*) So round about ten to nine this evening?

Celia Something like that. (*She regains control of herself, something of her
customary sharpness of manner returning*) I must say looking at my watch
wasn't the first thought on my mind.

Bruton No, of course not. It must have been a shock.

Celia It was, Inspector. I've only been married the once, so it is actually the
first time I've found my husband murdered.

Bruton I'm sorry. I'm not putting this very well. Given the trauma that
you've just suffered, Miss Wallis, it's presumably too early for you to have
a theory about what might have happened ... ?

Celia I don't need a theory. It's self-evident. Someone shot him.

Bruton I meant a theory about who that person might have been.

Celia I saw Martin's murderer.

Bruton looks up at her sharply

Earlier in the evening, there was a man lurking in the garden ...

Bruton Lurking?

Celia (*gesturing towards the front door*) I saw his silhouette through the
glass of that door.

Bruton Did you challenge him or anything?

Celia I called Martin. He opened the door and ——

Bruton And what?

Celia (*knowing it's an anti-climax*) And the man'd gone.

Bruton Hm. Who do you think it was?

Celia I don't know. Someone who wanted to steal money, someone high on
drugs perhaps. I don't know.

Bruton It is a statistical fact, Miss Wallis, that the vast majority of murders
are committed by people who know their victims.

Celia Well, this is an exciting day for you, Inspector, isn't it? Because today's
is one of the minority of murders.

Bruton What makes you so sure?

Celia Apart from anything else, no-one knew that Martin was coming
tonight except me.

Bruton Assuming of course that your husband was the intended victim ...

Celia He must have been.

Bruton Whoever wrote this letter seems to have it in for *you*, though,
wouldn't you say?

Celia looks shocked

Back to events of this evening; your husband's death. I hope you don't mind my asking, Miss Wallis — but what would you say was the state of your marriage?

Celia The state of our marriage? Dead from the neck up. And certainly dead from the waist down.

Bruton Not entirely happy then?

Celia (*sarcastically*) Nothing wrong with your deductive powers, is there, Inspector Bruton?

Bruton You and your husband no longer slept together?

Celia Inspector Bruton, it's a long time since Martin and I have slept under the same roof, let alone the same duvet.

Bruton But you were both here together this evening.

Celia I'm only here because it's convenient for Brighton where I'm working. I don't like this house. It has too many memories.

Bruton So, going back to the state of your marriage ...

Celia Martin and I had a marriage which was absolutely equal. He loathed me, and I loathed him. But that doesn't mean I murdered him.

Bruton looks at Celia suspiciously

(*Shocked by what she sees in his expression*) You actually do think of me as a suspect in Martin's murder?

Bruton The first suspect in any murder investigation is always the person who discovers the body.

Celia Is that another statistical fact?

Bruton Yes.

Celia shakes her head in disbelief

All I'm saying, Miss Wallis, is that it's very important we eliminate you from our enquiries as soon as possible.

Celia And what would "eliminate me from your enquiries"?

Bruton Well, let's say if you had an alibi, if you could prove that you were elsewhere at the time your husband was shot ...

Celia I do know what an alibi is.

Bruton Say you were out of the house; even better, say you were in the company of someone else who could vouch for that fact ...

Celia (*slightly bewildered, thinking it through*) No, I wasn't with anyone else — and I was actually here ...

Bruton That's rather a pity, from your point of view ...

Celia (*remembering*) I wasn't *with* anyone, but I was talking to a friend on the telephone.

Bruton This telephone?

Celia No, I was using the one in the kitchen.

Bruton Why?

Celia Because Martin had got his bloody music blaring out here and in the study.

Bruton That'd be the music that was on when we arrived?

Celia Yes.

Bruton Not my taste. I'm more of a Lloyd Webber man myself. Like something with a tune I can recognize. What was it, by the way?

Celia Some incidental music Martin was using for a production. *'Tis Pity She's a Whore.*

Bruton Sorry?

Leach It's the name of a play by John Ford.

Bruton And what's it about?

Leach Incest, sir.

Bruton Dear, oh dear. You can get away with anything in the name of entertainment these days, can't you?

Celia It was written in 1633.

Bruton Was it? Ah.

A particularly loud thump is heard from inside the study

Oh, for heaven's sake! Fisher!

Fisher (*appearing through the curtains*) Sir.

Bruton Could you keep the noise down? I am trying to conduct an interview in here.

Fisher Sorry, sir. (*He disappears back into the study, closing the curtains*)

Bruton So ... This phone call you were having in the kitchen, Miss Wallis: who was it to?

Celia My friend Gilly. You see, she was up for *The Boy Friend.*

Bruton (*not understanding*) Which boy friend would that be?

Celia The musical. I heard from my agent, Max Fenton — he's Gilly's agent too — that she'd got the part. So I was ringing her to say, "Well done."

Bruton Really? And you're close to this friend of yours, are you?

Celia Very. We spend hours nattering on the phone.

Bruton Good.

Celia Why "good"?

Bruton Because the longer you were in the kitchen nattering to your friend, Miss Wallis, the less time you would have had to be in the study.

Celia (*pleased*) Oh yes. Yes, I see. (*Suddenly cast down*) The trouble is this evening Gilly wasn't there. I talked to her answering machine.

Bruton Oh dear.

Celia And it was while I was leaving a message for her that I heard this noise like a gunshot, and then I came back in here and I ... (*She sobs*) I'm sorry ...

Bruton No, no, don't worry. I don't want to hurry you.

Celia But I want to be hurried. I want you to hurry up and eliminate me from your suspicions, so that you can concentrate on finding the man I saw lurking in the garden.

Bruton Right. OK, first things first. Give me your friend Gilly's number. Then we can check that you did actually make the call.

Celia Well, of course I did! It's in that address book. Under "Carnes". With a "C". That being her surname.

Bruton Thank you. (*He finds the entry in the address book and copies the number into his notebook*) Of course, there is one more thing that could speed up our investigations.

Celia What's that?

Bruton Fingerprints. If we found that no fingerprints of yours were on the murder weapon ... that would certainly shift suspicion away from you.

Celia (*excitedly*) Yes, yes, that's good.

Bruton The trouble is, I doubt whether we have your fingerprints on file ...

Celia (*mock-innocent*) Oh, surely they'll still be there from when I was investigated for dismembering my first husband with a machete ... ?

Bruton (*taking this straight*) I thought you said you'd only been married the once, Miss Wallis.

Celia I wasn't being entirely serious, Inspector. I gather a sense of humour's something else they don't teach you at Police College.

Bruton Not as part of the regular curriculum, no. Some people are not very keen on having their fingerprints taken. Regard it as an infringement of their civil liberties.

Celia I don't care about that.

Bruton Nor do I. (*With a dismissive chuckle*) Start worrying about civil liberties, and you've no idea how much you slow down police work.

Celia Can my fingerprints be done right away?

Bruton Yes. Come along. (*He moves towards the study*) One of the boys on the Scene of Crime team can ——

Celia I'm not going in there!

Bruton Of course not. Fisher!

Fisher (*appearing from the study*) Sir?

Bruton Fisher, would you take Miss Wallis out to the van?

Leach (*rising from her seat*) I could take her, sir, if you like.

Bruton No, Fisher'll do it. Come on, Fisher, hurry up.

Fisher Yes, sir.

Bruton (*handing the piece of paper with Gilly's phone number to Fisher*) And have this phone number checked out, will you.

Fisher Sir (*To Celia*) If you'd like to come with me, Madam ...

Celia Right.

Fisher opens the front door and moves to lead his charge off; Celia follows

Bruton So, Miss Wallis, can I just confirm ——

Celia and Fisher stop

—— your and your husband's marriage was not a happy one?

Celia Inspector Bruton, you're clearly not up with your gossip columns. Anyone could tell you that Martin and I despised each other, that we spent as little time together as humanly possible, and that we were about to get a divorce!

Celia exits regally into the garden with Fisher

Bruton I can take that as a "No" then, can I? Thank you. (*He closes the front door*)

Leach looks awkward. She knows Bruton's kept her back for some reason

So, Leach …

Leach Sir … ?

Bruton *Merchant of Venice* at Stratford, eh? I didn't know you were interested in the theatre.

Leach It's not a subject that often comes up at the station.

Bruton No. But you are familiar with the work of the late Martin Powell?

Leach (*enthusiastically*) I saw him in all his major roles. He was wonderful as ——

Bruton Did you ever meet Martin Powell?

Leach (*after an infinitesimal pause, looking at Bruton*) No, of course not, sir.

Bruton holds her look

(*Uncomfortable, looking away*) Shall I go and help them through in the study?

Bruton Yes. I'll call you when Miss Wallis comes back.

Leach Right you are, sir. (*She hurries through into the study*)

Bruton moves towards the front door. He inspects the opera cloak and floppy hat. He lifts up the cricket bag, weighs it in his hand, but does not open it

Neville Smallwood appears from the passage on to the landing upstairs. He is a journalist in his thirties. He looks fairly normal, but his manner is awkward, intense, at times unnervingly obsessive. He has just woken up from a drunken sleep, and stares around blearily. He is dressed in a very feminine dressing-gown of Celia's over his own shorts and socks

Neville (*calling out*) Do you know, I'm not sure that champagne and me quite see eye to eye.

Bruton reacts minimally to the sound. He does not move from the doorway, but listens impassively through the following monologue

(*Calling down to the kitchen*) Celia! I'll be with you in a minute. Soon as the room settles down a bit. (*He chuckles and looks at his watch*) I haven't been asleep as long as I thought. (*He starts to walk very gingerly down the stairs, keeping a firm hold on the banister*) Ooh, what people would say if they knew that I'd been sleeping in Celia Wallis's bed. They'd think I was a real … (*His words trickle away as he sees Inspector Bruton. He giggles*) Ah.

Bruton Good-evening.
Neville (*totally bewildered*) Good-evening.
Bruton And who might you be, may I ask?
Neville My name's Neville Smallwood.

Bruton looks at Neville impassively

(*Gabbling nervously*) I'm a journalist. A radio journalist. I'm here to interview Celia Wallis for tonight's Radio Two Arts Programme. She very rarely gives interviews and I'm honoured. I've been an admirer of hers for years and … (*His words trickle away once again. Then he becomes self-conscious about what he's wearing*) This isn't what I normally wear …

Bruton I'm glad to hear it.
Neville Normally it'd be more — suit, collar and tie, that sort of …
Bruton Yes.
Neville (*after a silence*) I'm sorry, but who are you?
Bruton (*taking out his identification and showing it to Neville*) I'm Inspector Bruton of the Sussex Police.
Neville Oh.
Bruton And I'd like to ask you a few questions, Mr Smallwood.
Neville Yes. Yes, of course. What, now?
Bruton I think it might be more appropriate if you got dressed, actually. You know, suit, collar and tie, that sort of thing …
Neville (*nodding*) Mm. Right. (*He turns, and starts to run up the stairs, then realizes running isn't a good idea for someone in his condition. He puts his hand to his head, and moves gingerly on up*) I'll see you in a moment then.

Bruton watches impassively as Neville goes up the stairs

Bruton One thing, Mr Smallwood …
Neville (*stopping at the entrance to the passage*) Yes?

Bruton If you were thinking of escaping from the balcony, I should warn you
that you won't get far.
Neville (*bewildered*) Why on earth should I want to escape? (*He looks
curiously at Bruton*)

*Bruton returns Neville's stare impassively. Neville is the first to break the eye
contact. He turns away*

Neville exits into the bedroom

Bruton goes through into the study, closing the doors behind him

*The front door opens, and Celia enters, wiping residual fingerprint ink off
her fingers with a tissue. Fisher looms in the doorway behind her*

Celia moves DS

Fisher Miss Wallis ...
Celia (*stopping, slightly apprehensive*) Yes.
Fisher There's something I have to ask you, Miss Wallis.
Celia Yes?

Fisher takes a notebook and pen out of his pocket and moves ponderously DS.
There is a moment of tension

Fisher (*holding his notebook forward*) Could I have your autograph?
Celia (*hugely relieved*) Yes, yes of course.
Fisher (*proffering the pen*) It's not for me, you understand. It's for the wife.
Celia (*signing*) Of course. (*She hands the notebook back*) There.
Fisher (*taking the notebook*) Thank you. (*He dares to be bold*) Actually, it's
not for the wife. I'm not married. I live on my own, actually. No, the
autograph's for me. I've always been ——

Bruton enters from the study. Fisher is instantly silent

Bruton (*looking suspiciously at Celia and Fisher*) Don't hang about, Fisher,
get on with it.

*Fisher gives a pleading look to Celia, begging her to say nothing about the
autograph*

Fisher (*mumbling*) Yes, sir. (*He shuffles past his boss into the study*)

Bruton Leach.

Leach comes silently through into the sitting-room. She sits down as before.
Throughout the ensuing scene, she watches Celia with focused intensity

Who's laughing boy in the bedroom then?

Celia (*remembering*) Oh, Lord, him. He's a journalist — radio journalist — called Neville Smallwood. I'd forgotten about him.

Bruton Do you normally forget what men there are in your bed, Miss Wallis?

Celia No. Normally I keep a very strict inventory. (*An awful new thought comes into her mind*) You didn't for one moment imagine that Neville and I ... ?

Bruton In my experience, when women have men in their beds, there is quite frequently some kind of — closeness between them.

Celia But — him? Inspector, when it comes to men, I shop at Harrods.

Bruton So Neville Smallwood ... ?

Celia Would hardly make it as a "Final Reduction" at a car boot sale. I mean, what do you take me for?

Bruton It's not my place to pass judgment, Miss Wallis, merely to form conclusions from the available facts. Your husband has been murdered, you admit your marriage was in a bad state, and that there was a man — not your husband — in a state of semi-undress in your bed. Until I'm offered another explanation, I think I could be excused for accepting the obvious one.

Celia Even when the obvious one totally fails to take into account the kind of woman I am?

Bruton (*stodgily*) I don't know what kind of woman you are, Miss Wallis.

Celia I am a woman with a strong sex-drive and exquisite taste. I don't end up in bed with sad losers.

Bruton But Mr Smallwood was in your bed. What was he doing there?

Celia I get many requests to do interviews.

Bruton But not in bed?

Celia (*snapping at Bruton*) No, not in bed!

Bruton Mr Smallwood implied that you very rarely gave interviews, Miss Wallis.

Celia With reason. All the tabloids want these days is dirt. You know: "FAMOUS STAR IN THREE-IN-A-BED ROMP."

Bruton Are you implying that there was someone else as well as Mr Smallwood in your bed?

Celia No! I was saying that in show business it's very hard to maintain any privacy.

Bruton So why did you agree to be interviewed by Mr Smallwood?

Celia He was very persistent.

Bruton You mean he pestered you?

Celia I wouldn't use the word "pestered". Though in fact my agent does call him "the Creepy-Crawly". Look, I'm opening in a new play in Brighton next week; it could use some publicity. Neville Smallwood is a journalist and a huge fan. I read the letters he wrote to my agent.

Bruton Were his letters typed?

Celia No, they were hand-written. Why do you ask?

Bruton The Stalker's letters were typewritten, weren't they?

Celia For heaven's sake! No, it's unthinkable that Neville had anything to do with those letters. Or with this murder. Apart from anything else, he was fast asleep at the moment Martin was shot.

Bruton How's that?

Celia Neville arrived at half-past seven this evening, as arranged, to do the interview. He's not, I'm afraid, God's gift to broadcasting. Still, he was perfectly amiable, so after we'd finished, I offered him a drink. In a very short time he was decidedly woozy — he's not used to drinking — so I took him up to my bedroom to sleep it off. End of story.

Bruton And he was asleep from then until he woke a few minutes ago?

Celia I assume so.

Bruton You didn't see him come back in here?

Celia No.

Bruton I noticed there's a balcony to the bedroom. And steps down from it.

Celia (*testily*) Yes, there is. Of course there is. (*She gestures towards the following as she speaks*) And there's a window in the bathroom. And a window in Martin's bedroom. And there's the front door, and a back door from the kitchen. And a murderer could have gone out of any one of them and got in through the french windows and shot Martin. But Neville Smallwood isn't a murderer!

Bruton Until we have proof that he isn't, Miss Wallis, he remains a suspect.

Celia As do I.

Bruton As do you, yes.

Celia (*suddenly breaking down*) Do you realize how awful this whole business is for me, Inspector, even without being accused of actually committing the crime? Have you any idea what it feels like to lose someone who's been part of your life for fifteen years?

Bruton (*formally*) I'm glad to say I've never had that experience.

Celia Well, I hope you never do. How is Mrs Bruton, by the way? And the two little Brutons?

Bruton All my family are fine, thank you.

Celia That's a novelty in the Police Force, isn't it? Notoriously bad profession for marriage breakdowns, so I've heard.

Bruton Yes, Miss Wallis. Just like the theatre. (*He moves towards the study and opens the curtains*) Fisher, how're we doing on finding the bullet?

Fisher We've located it. In the wall behind the dead man.

Bruton moves into the study and closes the curtains behind him

Leach Are you sure I can't get you anything, Miss Wallis?
Celia Quite sure, thank you. Have you worked with Inspector Bruton a lot?
Leach This is the first time.
Celia You'd have thought there'd be someone else available. Someone with
a modicum of sensitivity. (*She looks at Leach*) You seem to know a lot
about my husband's career.
Leach Yes. (*She looks at a picture on the wall*) That's him as Richard III.
Celia Did you see it?
Leach (*nodding*) He was very cruel ... but very charismatic.
Celia Yes. (*Looking intently at Leach*) You're not the typical image of a
policewoman, are you?
Leach (*after shaking her head*) I don't think I am.
Celia No.

There is a moment of tension between them; Leach breaks it

Leach If you'll excuse me then ... ?
Celia Of course.

Leach goes through into the study

Neville, now dressed in suit and tie, emerges on to the landing

Neville Psst!

Celia looks up towards Neville

Celia, what's going on? Why does that policeman want to ask me some
questions? (*He sways and puts his hand up to his head*)
Celia Are you all right?
Neville Sorry. A little bit wobbly. Not used to champagne.
Celia You'll soon feel better.
Neville (*suddenly looking at his watch*) Oh, has the courier come to take the
interview tape to the BBC? We haven't missed him, have we?
Celia No, no. It's not due to be picked up till nine-forty-five.
Neville Good. Because that interview's really important for me.

*Bruton enters from the study. From this moment on to the end of the act,
Bruton becomes less of the Mr Plod and more menacing as he turns his power
on Neville*

What's been going on here?

Bruton Exactly, Mr Smallwood. What *has* been going on here?

Neville Well, I'm sorry. I'm completely lost.

Bruton (*taking out his notebook*) Could I take a few personal details, please?
Your name is Neville Smallwood?

Neville Yes.

Bruton Address?

Neville 73 Braemar Drive, Rustington, West Sussex, BN16 2EF.

Bruton (*writing it down*) Thank you.

Neville (*alarmed*) You're not going to have to go round and see Mother, are
you? She's an old lady and I don't want her upset.

Bruton There will be no need for us to disturb your mother, Mr Smallwood.
At this point.

*Neville looks anxious at this veiled threat. Bruton tears the page out of his
notebook and goes back to the study doors. He opens one door and holds the
sheet of paper out*

Leach.

Leach (*coming into vision*) Sir.

Bruton gives Leach the paper

Bruton Usual checks, please.

Leach Yes, sir.

Bruton closes the door and turns back into the sitting-room

Neville Usual checks? What does that mean?

Bruton Purely routine, Mr Smallwood. Your details will be checked on the
police computer. To see if you have any previous convictions. And if you
don't have any previous convictions — (*he smiles blandly*) — then you
don't have anything to worry about, do you, Mr Smallwood?

Neville (*uneasily*) No ...

Celia Neville was simply here to interview me.

Bruton Yes, thank you, Miss Wallis. (*He focuses again on Neville*) Is that
your car parked in the drive? The brown Austin Maestro?

Neville Yes.

Bruton Could I have the keys, please?

Neville Keys?

Bruton Wouldn't like to be breathalysed, would you?

Neville No.

Neville hands the keys to Bruton

But I still don't understand ——

Bruton When a crime's been committed, the first thing we try to do is to narrow down the list of suspects. (*He moves back to the study, opening the curtains*) Fisher.

Fisher comes into sight in the study doorway

Here are the keys to the Maestro. Check it out, could you?

Bruton hands the car keys to Fisher

Fisher (*heading for the the exit*) Yes, sir.

Bruton comes back into the sitting-room, closing the study curtains behind him

Bruton And send Wilkins over.
Fisher Sir.

Fisher exits

Bruton (*to Neville*) Another thing we can do to help eliminate you from our enquiries, Mr Smallwood, is to check your fingerprints.
Neville I'm not a criminal.
Celia I've just had mine done. It's no big deal. It'll speed up the investigation.
Neville All right, you can take my fingerprints. See if I care. When do you want to do it?
Bruton No time like the present. (*He calls in the direction of the front garden*) Wilkins!

Wilkins appears

Could you do another set of fingerprints, please? It's Mr Smallwood.
Neville (*rather plaintively*) I wish someone would tell me what the hell's going on. What is the crime that you're investigating?
Bruton Oh, you really don't know? Well, I'll show you exactly the crime that we're investigating, Mr Smallwood! Look away, Miss Wallis!

Celia buries her head in her hands and remains with her back to the study. Bruton hurries across and theatrically pulls open the curtains. Martin's body is still in its chair, with a dust sheet thrown over him. The blood-spattered wall behind can still be seen. Neville stands very still, looking us

There, Mr Smallwood! That's the crime that's being investigated! Murder. The murder of Martin Powell. What do you say to that?

Neville (*after a little giggle*) Good.
Celia (*shocked*) What?

Neville has a burst of hysterical giggles, and then quite quickly recovers himself. Celia and Bruton watch in amazement

Neville (*casually, as if nothing had happened*) Right, shall we get these fingerprints done?
Bruton Go with Wilkins to the van, and it'll all be sorted out very quickly.
Wilkins If you'd come this way, Mr Smallwood ...

Neville, with a strange, almost smug, smile on his face, goes out of the front door with Wilkins

Bruton turns back to Celia. Leach sits, watching Celia intently

Bruton (*with a slight shudder*) What a weirdo. Are you still telling me that guy's normal?
Celia Well, he's — perhaps eccentric.
Bruton You have a way with words, Miss Wallis. He's a complete basket case. (*He goes back into interrogation mode*) What time did your husband arrive here this evening?
Celia Eight o'clock — quarter past, perhaps.
Bruton You were expecting him?
Celia He arrived a bit earlier than he'd said, but, yes, I was expecting him.
Bruton Why was he coming down? So that the two of you could spend a pleasant domestic evening together?
Celia Any time we spent together wasn't domestic, it was gladiatorial.
Bruton Ah.
Celia In fact, Martin was coming down this evening so that we could have a serious talk about the next step towards actually getting divorced. Martin has a new girlfriend. He's had lots of girlfriends in the past. Rather predatory with women. Always picking up adoring fans at the stage door — called them his "Stage Door Jennies", I'm afraid.
Bruton And did he form relationships with these women?
Celia Yes. If ten minutes in his dressing room qualifies as a relationship.
Bruton Ah.
Celia No, none of those really counted. But the latest girlfriend, Victoria, is apparently more serious. He actually wants — wanted — to marry her.
Bruton Have you met the young lady in question?
Celia I've seen her work.

Bruton looks quizzical

On stage.

Bruton Oh, another actress.

Celia Only just, in her case.

Bruton Are you suggesting she's not a very talented actress?

Celia I've seen more animation in a brick. Victoria is a very tiny talent in a very tiny person.

Bruton She's short, you mean?

Celia If she were ever cast as Snow White, the Seven Dwarfs would feel really threatened.

Bruton But, in spite of all this, your husband was proposing to marry the young lady?

Celia Yes. Hence the more focused talk of divorce.

Bruton Presumably that's rather upsetting for you, Miss Wallis. Bit of a slap in the face, isn't it?

Celia You mean I should be jealous? The time for jealousy in my marriage is long past. I don't care what Martin does — (*she corrects herself, momentarily emotional*) — I mean I had long since ceased to care what he did. If he'd found some bimbo who wanted to marry him ... Well, actually his death has saved her from a great deal of unhappiness, so it's not all bad news, is it?

Bruton Did Mr Smallwood meet your husband this evening, Miss Wallis?

Celia Yes.

Bruton Did they hit it off? Was there an instant affinity between them?

Celia Hardly. Neville is very much not Martin's type. I'm afraid my husband never developed the skill of suffering fools gladly.

Bruton Ah. Of course, I never met Mr Powell.

Celia Probably just as well then.

Bruton reacts to the implied insult

And when they did meet, Neville didn't help the situation.

Bruton Oh?

Celia Look, Neville's besotted with me ...

Bruton Is he?

Celia (*trying to make it sound less suspicious*) No, not besotted in a real way. Just besotted as a fan. He'd read various gossip column accounts of our marriage breakdown, and he reckoned that I was the injured party. So, confronted by the man who, to his mind, had caused me so much pain, I'm afraid Neville Smallwood, in his own rather bizarre way, let rip at my husband.

Bruton "Let rip at your husband"? You mean they had a row?

Celia Not a row as such. Just a disagreement. It was nothing. It didn't last.

Bruton I see. But he was pleased to see that your husband's dead, wasn't he?

Celia has no answer to this. Bruton is now near the front door, and takes the opera cloak and floppy hat off the pegs there

Planning on going to a fancy dress party, Miss Wallis?

Celia Those aren't mine. They're Neville's.

Bruton (*trying on the cloak and hat*) Really? Funny, I wouldn't have put him down as the flamboyant type.

Celia He's obsessed with the theatre, Inspector. He thinks going round in a cloak and hat like that makes him look like one of us.

Bruton Whereas, in fact ...

Celia It makes him look a complete prat.

Bruton Yes.

Celia As it does you.

Bruton Thank you. (*He takes off the cloak and hat, hangs them up, and looks down again at the long cricket bag*) Would this be Mr Smallwood's bag down here?

Celia Yes, he had it with him when he arrived.

Bruton Ah. (*He lifts the bag up*) I wouldn't have reckoned on him as the sporting type either. Can't see Neville Smallwood saving England's innings with a timely century, can you?

Celia No.

Bruton Large bag, isn't it?

Celia He brought it because he thought we'd need a microphone on a stand. I told him it wasn't necessary. We could just sit on the sofa with the cassette recorder on the table. Quite honestly, I got the feeling I'd had rather more experience of radio interviews than Neville had. In fact, I wondered whether he'd ever done one before.

Bruton Hm. (*He places the bag on the sofa. He unzips the bag and looks down into it*) This is not my idea of a microphone stand. (*Very deliberately, he takes the rubber gloves out of his pocket and puts them on. Then he reaches into the bag and pulls out a Wild West-style rifle. He weighs it in his hands*) Not my idea of a microphone stand at all. (*He turns to Leach*) Look like a microphone stand to you, does it, Leach?

Leach No, sir.

Bruton Who does it belong to?

Celia Well, it belongs to ... It did belong to ... (*Apologetically*) It belongs to Neville. But only just.

Bruton Only just? I'd have thought being the owner of something was a bit like being pregnant. You either are or you aren't.

Celia I meant "only just" in the sense that I only gave it to him this evening.

Bruton You gave it to him? And what words did you use as you handed it across? "I thought you might like this — oh, and by the way, would you mind shooting my husband with it ... ?"

Celia No, I didn't say that! It goes back to *Annie Get Your Gun*.

Bruton *Annie Get Your Gun?*

Celia The musical.

Bruton Ah, you mean … (*He sings*) "Oh, the Deadwood Stage is comin' on over the hill …"

Leach I think you'll find that's *Calamity Jane*, sir.

Bruton Ah.

Leach *Annie Get Your Gun* is "No Business Like Show Business", "Doin' What Comes Natur'lly", "You Can't Get A Man With A Gun" … Music and Lyrics by Irving Berlin. Book by Herbert and Dorothy Fields. Betty Hutton in the movie, not Doris Day.

Celia Very good, Leach.

Bruton (*testily*) All right, all right. I know the show you mean. What's it to do with this?

Celia *Annie Get Your Gun* was my first job. Straight out of drama school. At the Leicester Haymarket.

Bruton And it was during that production that you first met Neville Smallwood?

Celia I didn't meet him, but he did see the show. He saw it many times. I only found out this evening, as it happens. I think I became part of his fantasies.

Bruton His sick fantasies.

Celia No. Neville's enthusiasm is entirely harmless. *Annie Get Your Gun* was his first experience of the theatre. He fell in love with the show. And he fell in love with me. That's when he started his Celia Wallis Collection. He sought out all kinds of memorabilia about me and the show. Do you know, he even persuaded the management to give him a life-size cut-out of me as Annie Oakley that they'd had done for publicity?

Bruton And you're still trying to tell me that these were the actions of someone normal?

Celia They were the actions of a fan.

Bruton And that excuses everything, does it? As I recall, the guy who shot John Lennon described himself as "a fan". Sounds like classic obsessive behaviour to me.

Celia Anyway, Neville told me all this this evening, and so — I gave him the gun.

Bruton You gave him the gun?

Celia Yes. It was up there, mounted on the wall, and he seemed so interested in everything about the show that — I just gave it to him.

Bruton Do you have a licence for this, Miss Wallis?

Celia No. It's a souvenir, a stage prop. It's not really a gun.

Bruton (*looking at the rifle*) Looks pretty much like one to me.

Celia It fires blanks.

Bruton Only blanks?

Celia The ones we used onstage were, obviously.

Bruton But were there others? *(Pause)* You'd better tell me, Miss Wallis.

Celia We did a charity thing at a rifle range in Leicester. We used real bullets for that.

Bruton And do you still have those real bullets?

Celia I honestly can't remember.

Bruton *(clearly not believing her)* Hm. *(He reaches into the cricket bag and produces a Western-style leather ammunition belt)* Recognize this? *(During the following he carefully removes a bullet from the belt and looks at it closely)*

Celia Yes. It was part of my Annie Oakley costume.

Bruton And did you give this to Mr Smallwood as well?

Celia Yes. Along with the knife and the ——

Bruton I'm rather afraid your memory's played you false, Miss Wallis. *(He holds up the bullet)* This one isn't a blank.

Celia Oh dear.

Bruton moves to the study holding the rifle and belt gingerly in his gloved hands and opens the curtain

Bruton Give me a couple of evidence bags, Carter.

Carter approaches and gives Bruton two evidence bags. Bruton puts the rifle and ammunition belt in them

Fisher.

Fisher Sir?

Bruton Have Wilkins get these tested for fingerprints.

Fisher Yes, sir.

Bruton And have the rifle checked against the murder bullet.

Fisher exits

Now, Miss Wallis ——

A mobile phone rings in Bruton's pocket

(Answering the phone) Bruton. ... Oh yes. Right. ... Oh. Did you actually hear the noise on the tape? ... Hm. ... OK. Thanks. *(He switches off the mobile phone, returns it to his pocket, and looks across at Celia)* Well, well ...

Celia Well, well what?

Bruton One of my men has been checking with your friend Gilly Carnes.

Your message was on her answering machine ——
Celia (*justified*) Thank you.
Bruton — and, recorded in the background of what you're saying, there is a muffled bang. We'll have to check it out further, but if it is identified as a gunshot, then that would seem to eliminate you as a suspect ——
Celia See! That's what I said, didn't I?
Bruton — provided there's no fingerprint evidence against you.

Celia looks exasperated

Going back to the Stalker's original letters ...
Celia Mm?
Bruton You don't still have any of them, do you?
Celia Well, yes, I do, actually.
Bruton But in London, presumably?
Celia No, he sent some of them here. (*She goes to the sitting-room desk and looks for the letters*)
Bruton I'd just like to compare them with the most recent one. Incidentally, why do you keep them, Miss Wallis? I thought those letters represented one of the most terrifying times of your life.

Celia finds a letter and hands it to Bruton

Celia Yes, but — well, they are quite flattering. You won't find many actresses who'll destroy a good review.
Bruton (*looking at the letter*) Even if it comes from a certifiable psychopath?
Celia We don't know that's what he was. You never found him, did you?
Bruton (*angered by this reminder*) No. (*With renewed vigour*) Which means that he's still at large. (*He looks at the letter*) This stuff's really creepy. (*He reads a passage at random*)

During Bruton's following reading, the front door opens and Neville returns, wiping ink from his fingers with a tissue. Quietly closing the door, he stands US, *listening*

"Celia Wallis, your talent is not of this time, but of all time. Perhaps only in death can you be truly mine. Your death will only make you live more brightly, for the flame of your talent will still burn in my heart. You are the lodestone of my life.

Neville joins in, quoting from memory

Bruton⎫ (*together*) "Towards you, dead or alive, I will always return ... "
Neville⎭

Bruton's voice trickles away; he, Celia and Leach turn round and look, fascinated, at Neville

Neville (*as if repeating some religious rite*) "And whenever I seem to have vanished off your horizon, do not fear. I will not have gone for ever. I will be only waiting, waiting to return, to claim your talent and your beauty, to claim them as my own."

There is a long silence at the end of Neville's recitation. Finally, Bruton breaks it

Bruton You seem to have a good grasp of that from memory.

Neville Of course.

Bruton You're not denying that you wrote it then?

Neville Why should I? (*To Celia*) I'm just so flattered to know that you kept them. I'd thought you would have thrown them away long ago.

Celia (*confusedly*) Well, no, I ...

Neville (*seeing his bag*) What's my bag doing here?

Bruton (*picking up the recent letter*) And what about this letter, Mr Smallwood? Recognize this at all? (*He reads*) "And when our blood commingles, you will be mine forever. When my knife traces the soft contours of your skin —— "

Neville I didn't write that.

Bruton (*disbelievingly*) Really? Leach, will you go and check if we've got anything from the computer yet?

Leach Yes, sir.

Leach exits through the front door, closing it

Bruton starts getting increasingly aggressive and building up the pressure on Neville

Bruton Mr Smallwood, I gather you had a bit of a shouting match with Mr Powell earlier this evening.

Neville I made no secret of what I thought of him, no.

Bruton And then what happened?

Neville Well, I — I'm afraid the alcohol got the better of me. I sort of passed out.

Bruton Convenient stuff, alcohol, isn't it?

Neville "Convenient"? So far as I'm concerned, it was very inconvenient. I was interviewing Celia for the Radio Two Arts ——

Leach enters, holding a computer printout in her hand

Bruton Yes?
Leach The printout, sir.

Bruton takes the printout from Leach

Bruton Thank you.

Leach sits down unobtrusively. Bruton comes DS, *reading the printout. He gives Neville a piercing look*

Bruton Well, well, well, Mr Smallwood ... You are a dark horse, aren't you?
Neville I don't know what you mean.
Bruton (*consulting the printout*) Do you remember what happened on the sixth of April twelve years ago?
Neville (*sullenly*) No.
Bruton Funny, I'd've thought it was the kind of thing that would stick in a person's mind—appearing at Worthing Magistrates' Court, being severely reprimanded and fined fifty pounds ...

Neville looks downcast

I never think it's a very pleasant crime, that — stealing women's under-wear from a washing line.

Celia looks at Neville with new distaste

Do you know what we in the police call men who do that? Knicker-nickers. Rather amusing, isn't it: knicker-nicker?

But Neville is not amused

I often wonder what makes a man do that sort of thing — not a sign of a very healthy mind, I'd say.
Neville (*petulantly defensive*) It was a long time ago. I was very young and confused.
Bruton Yes. I bet you were. But I dare say you've grown out of that sort of behaviour now, haven't you?

Neville is silent

Still, let's return to more recent events. The events of earlier this evening. What you want me to believe, Mr Smallwood, is that, after your little verbal set-to with Mr Powell, you passed out on Miss Wallis's bed, and remained there blissfully asleep until you suddenly stumbled out on to the landing in Miss Wallis's dressing-gown and saw me?

Neville Yes. That's what happened.

Bruton Let me tell you what I think happened, Mr Smallwood. I don't think you did pass out from alcohol, you see. I think you pretended to, you appeared to. But then, when Miss Wallis wasn't around, when she'd gone off to make a telephone call, you slipped down from the balcony, collected your bag, re-entered the house, took the rifle she'd given you, and came into this study.

Neville I've never been in that study!

Bruton I think you have, Mr Smallwood. And I'm sure we can prove you have. There'll be something in here with your fingerprints on. Just as I'm sure we'll find them all over the rifle you used to shoot Martin Powell!

Neville Celia! Stop him. He's talking nonsense.

Celia Inspector Bruton, what you're suggesting is ridiculous.

Bruton Is it? I don't think so. Neville Smallwood has obligingly identified himself as our missing Stalker, he's admitted he hated your husband, he had the gun, he had the ammunition. Motive, means, opportunity — what more do you want?

Celia I want you to catch the person who actually committed the murder.

Bruton So do I. But trouble is, in this case I'm getting rather low on suspects. You seem to have been cleared by the telephone message to your friend. So who does that leave? Detective Sergeant Fisher?

Fisher (*amazed*) What?

Bruton He's a fan of yours, certainly, but a rather more restrained one than Mr Smallwood. (*He advances menacingly on Neville*) Fisher's not obsessive. He's not a knicker-nicker. He's not sick. He's not unhinged.

Celia Inspector Bruton, why do you keep bullying him?

Bruton Why? I'll show you exactly why!

Bruton hustles Celia up to face the study and draws the curtains back. Martin's body, with no sheet over it, is revealed. The Scene of Crime Team look out at Celia

That's why, Miss Wallis! Because your husband's been murdered!

Celia lets out a gut-wrenching scream at the sight of her husband's body. She turns away DS, *destroyed*

(*Turning to Fisher*) Fisher, you come with me. I'm going to need your help.

Fisher nods and goes out through the french windows

(*Picking up the champagne flute*) And I think it could be interesting to get a few fingerprints off this.

Bruton goes out of the french windows

Neville stands in a state of shock; Celia is still appalled

Celia Please ... Shut it out.

The Scene of Crime team close the study curtains. Neville moves numbly DS and sinks on to the sofa. Leach stays onstage; she gets up and seems to be looking nonchalantly at the posters, but is actually listening all the time

Neville If I had done it, Celia, what would you think?
Celia (*coming out of her state of shock*) I beg your pardon?
Neville Would you be proud of me?
Celia Proud of you?
Neville Would you think I'd been brave, even heroic, you know, to save you from that monster?
Celia No. No, Neville, I don't think that would be my reaction.
Neville (*disappointedly*) Oh.
Celia Neville, you would have committed murder. I'm afraid I don't think committing murder is ever brave or heroic.
Neville Even when the victim is pure evil, and is causing great unhappiness to someone you love?
Celia Even then.
Neville (*once again disappointedly*) Oh. (*With a funny little laugh*) Just as well I didn't murder your husband then, isn't it? I wouldn't have got the reaction from you that I was hoping for.
Celia (*looking at him curiously*) No. You wouldn't.
Neville Oh, well, no harm done. I'll know another time, won't I?
Celia (*incredulously*) What?
Neville I'll know another time that murder isn't the way to your heart. (*He looks at her very fixedly*) But don't worry, Celia. Martin's gone now — and you will be mine.

Celia stares at him, appalled

(*Responding to Celia's stare*) That is a joke, Celia. That was just my little joke.
Celia (*not entirely convinced*) Yes. Yes, of course. (*She sees Leach, and takes this as an excuse to rise, perhaps too hastily, from the sofa*) All right if I go and make some coffee?
Leach I'll come with you.

They go off into the kitchen. Neville looks rather mournfully around the room. Then he looks around with more enthusiasm

Neville Don't be down in the dumps, Neville. Martin Powell is dead, and you are actually in Celia Wallis's house. (*His attention is caught by the "Annie Get Your Gun" knife on the wall of weapons. He moves across, reaches up and takes it down. He holds it reverently for a moment, then unsheathes it and feels the blade. He lets out a little giggle, puts the knife back into its sheath and slips it into his pocket. Prompted by the memory, he sings a brief snatch of "There's No Business Like Show Business" from "Annie Get Your Gun'" and goes into some long-remembered steps of choreography. There is something slightly sinister about his performance. The choreography leaves him bowing virtually over the coffee table. He sees the sheet of notes and the cassette recorder beneath them. Neville picks up the cassette recorder and looks at it. The blinking red light's on*) Good heavens. It's still on. (*He presses the "stop" button, then the "rewind". After a few seconds, he stops it and presses the "play"*)

A piece of the recording is heard

Neville's Voice — no harm done. I'll know another time, won't I?
Celia's Voice What?
Neville's Voice I'll know another time that murder isn't the way to your heart. That ——

Neville presses the "stop" button on the recorder. He does not press the "rewind", but, with fumbling hands, takes out the cassette. He hurries across to his cricket bag, puts the cassette recorder into it, and produces a carefully labelled Jiffy bag and a stapler. He pops the cassette into the Jiffy bag and staples it closed. At the sound of the front door opening, Neville puts the Jiffy bag down guiltily on a table

Bruton enters, looks suspiciously at Neville, and is about to say something when the kitchen door opens ——

Celia enters, carrying a tray of coffee. Leach follows her

Celia I've made some coffee, Inspector. Would you like a cup?
Bruton No, thank you. A motorbike courier has just arrived from the BBC. Were you expecting someone?
Celia Yes. He's come for the tape of the interview we did earlier, and for some publicity material the producer asked for. (*She crosses to the desk, and picks up the labelled Jiffy bag, larger than the one Neville had*) Have you got the tape, Neville?
Neville All labelled up. (*He picks the smaller Jiffy bag up off the table, and moves to hand it to Celia*)

Celia takes the smaller Jiffy bag and puts it into the larger one

Bruton Just a minute. I want to know what's in that bag.
Neville Oh, for God's sake! It's the tape.

Bruton, ignoring Neville, takes the large Jiffy bag from Celia, and removes from it the smaller Jiffy bag, along with some sheets of biographical material and photographs of Celia. He rips open the smaller Jiffy bag and inspects the cassette during the following

You have no right to open that.
Celia Don't antagonize him, Neville. He's only doing his job.
Neville And he's ruining my chances of doing my job. This interview's my big break and ——
Bruton Yes. That appears to be in order. It's a tape.
Neville (*sarcastically*) Not much gets past you, does it, Inspector? What the hell did you think I might have put in it?
Bruton It could have been an attempt by you to remove some incriminating evidence from the scene of the crime.
Neville Well, I don't see why that should worry you. Be a matter of moments for someone of your skills to manufacture a bit more, wouldn't it?
Bruton Mr Smallwood, being offensive is not going to help your cause.

Neville puts the contents back into the large Jiffy bag and staples it

Leach.
Leach Sir?

Bruton takes the package from Neville and hands it to Leach

Bruton Give this to the courier and sign the chitty.
Leach (*moving to the front door*) Very good, sir.
Bruton And tell Fisher he's going to be needed in a moment.

Leach goes out, closing the door behind her

Neville (*nervously*) What's Fisher going to be needed for?
Bruton Oh, don't worry, Mr Smallwood. I'm not going to set him on you — much though Fisher himself might enjoy that. No, in fact, Fisher's going to help us with a little reconstruction of the apparition that you, Miss Wallis, claim to have seen outside the front door.
Celia I don't *claim* to have seen it. I saw it.
Bruton You don't have to protect him, you know.

Celia (*shocked*) What?

Bruton I wouldn't imagine you meet a great many criminals in your line of work, Miss Wallis.

Celia No, of course not.

Bruton And you probably have some image that criminals are like the ones in the plays you do, in the television series you take part in: flamboyant figures, frightening figures, even rather glamorous figures ...

Celia I wouldn't have said ——

Bruton Well, they're not! I've met a great many criminals in my time — (*he suddenly and ferociously advances on Neville; by the end of the speech he is very close to Neville and almost shouting in his face*) — and most of them're just pathetic social misfits, inadequates who can't cope with life and who turn to crime because they are incapable of doing anything else!

Neville (*with a kind of quiet dignity*) And that's how you see me, is it, Inspector?

Bruton (*calming down a little*) Until you convince me there's another way of seeing you, Mr Smallwood, yes, I'm rather afraid it is.

Neville Must be your lucky day — because I've got so much going for me, haven't I? Goodness, if you'd actually been searching for a patsy to pin this murder on, you'd have been hard pressed to find someone more suitable. There's my previous conviction, for a start. That must mean I'm an oddball, mustn't it?

Bruton Mr Smallwood, normal people don't steal underwear from clothes lines.

Neville And there's no chance that I'm normal, is there? I don't live on my own, but I live with my mother. That's not normal. I must be "funny", mustn't I?

Bruton You said it.

Neville Just because you live with your mother, you know, it doesn't automatically make you a psychopath. But you think it does. Because you've done courses about Psychological Profiling. So when you've got a nice juicy murder on your hands, all you do is to find the saddest person you can and immediately arrest them. What you don't realize is that for every ten thousand people who've got posters of Charles Manson and collections of hard-core pornography involving dogs, there's probably only one who ever even contemplates the idea of murdering someone.

Bruton (*after a pause*) Do you have a collection of hard-core pornography involving dogs?

Neville (*sneeringly defiant*) Why? Do you want to borrow some?

Bruton No, thank you. (*After a pause*) You still haven't answered my question. *Do* you have a collection of hard-core pornography involving dogs?

Neville No, of course I don't!

Bruton (*disappointedly*) Oh.

Neville "Oh" meaning "pity", because then it'd be even easier to nail me, wouldn't it? Profile me, pigeonhole me. Loner at school; didn't play sport; no regular girlfriends; lives with his mother ... Well, you can supply the rest, can't you? Obviously, whatever's been done, I did it. God, I wish my job was as easy as yours.

Bruton Shut up!

Neville Do you realize, if everyone with the right profile actually became a serial killer, soon there'd be no-one left!

Bruton Thank you. Have you finished your little "Hearts and Flowers" routine? May we put away our handkerchiefs and get on with this reconstruction? Right. I think we can start. (*He opens the front door*) So, Miss Wallis, you say you saw the silhouette of a man —— ?

Celia A man with a hat on.

Bruton A man with a hat on, fine — through the frosted glass panel of this door. (*He steps in and out through the doorway*) So you called to your husband, but when he opened the door, there was no-one there?

Celia That's what he said, yes.

Neville The murderer could still have been lurking out of sight in the garden, waiting his moment to come in and shoot Mr Powell.

Bruton (*patronizingly*) Thank you, Mr Smallwood. He could have been. And all this time you were upstairs, dead to the world.

Neville I was!

Bruton Were you really, Mr Smallwood?

Neville Why don't you ask the people at Lodge Cottage if they saw anything?

Bruton I can assure you we've done that, Mr Smallwood. (*He looks out into the garden*) It's so dark out here, Miss Wallis, I'm surprised you could see any kind of outline. Was the exterior light on?

Celia It was earlier in the evening, Inspector. It hadn't got fully dark.

Bruton No, no, of course not. Well, I'm sure we can improvize something with car headlights. (*A thought strikes him*) Ooh, a man with a hat ... (*He takes Neville's hat from its peg, and speaks with heavy irony*) Mr Smallwood, I wonder if you'd be so kind as to lend us your hat, in the cause of police investigation ... ? It would be very public-spirited of you.

Neville And it might also give the impression that the intruder looked like me.

Bruton (*mock-innocent*) Good Lord, do you think it might? The idea had never occurred to me. Thank you so much for your co-operation, Mr Smallwood. (*He goes to the front door and calls out into the garden*) Fisher, we're nearly ready for the reconstruction.

Fisher (*off*) OK, sir.

Bruton Leach.

Leach follows Bruton off, closing the front door behind him. Celia looks scared at being alone with Neville

Celia (*after a nervous pause*) You didn't kill Martin, did you, Neville?

Neville (*advancing menacingly on Celia, putting a hand into his pocket*) For Christ's sake! You're not on Bruton's side too, are you?

Celia (*terrified*) No. All I want to do is to get at the truth. Look, Neville, it's not ——

Bruton enters through the front door. He leaves the door open

Bruton Mr Smallwood, Wilkins, my fingerprint chap, has done a preliminary check on the champagne glass found in Mr Powell's study and on the rifle that was used to kill him. He'll have to go to the lab to confirm his findings, but so far he's got a pretty good match on both items ... with the fingerprints you just gave him.

Neville Well, I certainly handled the rifle. Celia gave it to me.

Bruton Did you load it?

Neville I ... I don't see that I have to answer that question.

Bruton Don't you? Miss Wallis, did Mr Smallwood load the rifle?

Celia (*wretchedly*) Yes, Neville did load it.

Bruton And then what did he do with it?

Celia I'm not sure that this is relevant.

Bruton (*thundering*) What did he do with the rifle?

Celia (*unwillingly*) He threatened my husband with it.

Bruton He threatened your husband with it? (*He turns again to Neville*) Well, well, Mr Smallwood ... you know, even if I wanted to take a charitable view of your actions, you don't make things easy for me.

Neville is sullenly silent

So, at least we have an explanation for your fingerprints on the rifle. The glass, though, is something else again, isn't it — if you still insist that you didn't enter Mr Powell's study.

Bruton stares accusingly at Neville, who looks defiant, but is once again the first to drop his glance

(*Calling out into the garden*) Give it two minutes, Fisher, then go for it. (*He comes back into the room, closing the front door behind him, then moves* DS, *rubbing his hands together cheerfully*) So we're nearly set. Set to see the mysterious intruder. Quite exciting, isn't it?

Neville (*drily*) Is it?

Bruton Different people get excited by different things, Mr Smallwood ... but I'm sure I don't need to tell you that. Right now, was there as much light on the scene then as there is now, Miss Wallis? Had you got all of these lamps and things on?

Celia No. Martin had turned off all the lights.

Bruton So in here it was pitch dark, eh?

Celia The kitchen door was open, and some light was spilling through the curtain from the study.

Bruton Fine. Do you think we could recreate that lighting effect? Mr Smallwood, would you be kind enough to do the honours?

Neville crosses silently and truculently to the study doors, and opens one a little. A lot of light spills out from the police lights

(*Calling out*) Could we kill the spotlights in there, please? Just leave the desk lamp.

Carter and Wilkins turn off the spotlights; the light spill from the study is reduced

Thank you. Maybe you'd turn off the lights in here, Miss Wallis.

Celia does as she's told. The only light on the sitting-room is now what spills out from the study. With no back-lighting, nothing can be seen the other side of the frosted pane in the front door

(*To Celia*) And would you say that was the right amount of light? Or was the curtain open a bit wider? Not so wide perhaps?

Celia Not so wide.

Bruton Mr Smallwood ... ?

Neville slowly closes the study curtains during the following

Do say "when", Miss Wallis.

Celia (*when the spill of light is very narrow*) When.

Neville leaves the curtains where they have reached

Bruton Excellent. Now come and sit down and watch the spectacle, both of you.

Celia and Neville sit, facing the front door

(*Playing the scene slowly, relishing its drama*) Fisher will shortly be placing himself close up against the front door. Great fan of yours, Miss Wallis, Detective Sergeant Fisher is. But I mentioned that, didn't I?

Celia doesn't respond

He's even got a photograph of you stuck on his locker door, you know. And
Leach is a fan of your late husband. Coincidence, that, isn't it? And the
music was playing, is that right?
Celia Yes.

Bruton switches on the music

Bruton In a moment the headlights will beam across and we'll see Fisher in
all his glory. In all his *hatted* glory. In just a moment ——

*Apart from the music, there is a long, tense silence. Then, suddenly, car
headlights are switched on to outline for a moment a silhouette in the frosted
panel of the front door — the head and shoulders of a figure with a hat on.
Celia gasps. Bruton goes round the room, switching the lights back on. The
headlights are switched off; without back-lighting, nothing can be seen
behind the glass panel*

Bruton So — is that what it looked like, Miss Wallis?
Celia Yes.
Bruton Is that what you saw earlier this evening?
Celia (*subdued*) Yes.
Bruton (*switching off the music*) It was exactly like that?
Celia Yes.
Bruton Speaking as an actress, wouldn't you say it was a good performance
by Detective Sergeant Fisher? Very convincing impression of a murderous
intruder, eh?
Celia Yes.
Bruton Well, I think you should tell Fisher that to his face. (*He moves
towards the front door*) I'm sure he'd appreciate a compliment from
someone who knows as much about show business as you do. (*He pauses,
with his hand on the front door handle*) How about a nice round of applause
for the DS? Come on, Fisher — take your bow!

*Bruton opens the front door with a dramatic gesture to reveal — a life-size
cut-out of the younger Celia Wallis, dressed in her buckskin costume and
cowboy hat as Annie Oakley from "Annie Get Your Gun"!*

Recognize this, Mr Smallwood?
Neville Yes, it's from my Celia Wallis collection.
Bruton And you brought it here tonight, didn't you, along with all the other
things you brought that had any connection with the woman who has
obsessed you for years. And you used it to help you commit a murder.
Neville No. You've got it all wrong.

Bruton I don't think I have. You planned this whole thing. You imagined, in your sick mind, that killing her husband would somehow endear you to your idol. You staged your drunkenness. You set up this cut-out to make her think there was an intruder in the garden. You got out of the bedroom window and came into Martin Powell's study, where you shot him in cold blood.

Neville All wrong. All wrong.

Bruton I've got proof, or I will have very soon. We have your fingerprints on the rifle and the glass. Don't worry, I'll have quite enough evidence to arrest you, Mr Smallwood.

Neville You reckon?

Bruton Yes, I reckon.

Neville (*with a sudden dart to the kitchen door*) Well, you'll have to catch me first!

Wilkins enters, blocking Neville's path to the kitchen. Neville reaches into his pocket and produces the "Annie Get Your Gun" knife. He throws away the sheath and, with the knife in his hand, makes for the study doors

Leach enters through the study doors, barring Neville's way

Neville rushes up the stairs to the landing

Fisher enters on the landing, confronting Neville

Bruton Disarm him, Fisher!

Neville makes a lunge at Fisher with the knife. Fisher grabs Neville's arm and they struggle. Fisher bangs Neville's wrist on the banister, so that he drops the knife, which clatters down into the sitting-room. Fisher immobilizes Neville. Bruton picks up the knife

Just immobilize him, Fisher; no need for anything else.

Fisher frogmarches Neville downstairs to face Bruton

You won't get away that easily, Mr Smallwood. And you certainly won't get away in court. You killed Martin Powell, and for that crime you're going to go down for a long, long time!

Neville (*appealing to Celia; tearfully*) Celia! Celia!

But Neville is dragged away by Fisher. Wilkins goes through into the study. Leach lingers in the study doorway

Bruton You know, Miss Wallis, our professions are very different, yours
and mine ... but I bet we both feel the same sense of satisfaction when we
know we've got something right.

Celia You have no cause for satisfaction right now, Inspector. Because
you're wrong.

Bruton I'll be the judge of that.

Celia And the jury?

Bruton Yes, Miss Wallis. And the jury. (*He makes for the front door*)

Celia You got pleasure out of that. You bastard.

Bruton Just doing my job, Miss Wallis. (*He realizes he still has the knife in
his hand, and holds it out to her*) Yours, I believe.

Celia wordlessly takes the knife

*Bruton goes out without looking back at Celia. Leach follows and Bruton
shuts the front door behind them*

Celia collapses in shock, holding the knife and sobbing furiously

The CURTAIN *falls*

ACT II

The same. Half-past seven the same evening

The scene is more or less the same as it was for Act I, with the following changes: Martin's body is not on stage and the wall behind his desk is clean; there is a vase on the study desk and another, with flowers in it, on the mantelpiece (this, in Act I, was in the "Variety Club Award" niche); the cloak, raincoat and two hats are not hanging from the row of pegs; Neville's cricket bag is not on stage either; the glass doors to the study are closed; the coffee table in front of the sofa is uncluttered, except for some flowers (the tape machine and papers have gone); the "Annie Get Your Gun" rifle, ammunition belt and knife are in their positions on the wall, Martin Powell's "Variety Club Award" (a "Golden Heart") is also in its proper display niche

When the CURTAIN *rises, the sky beyond the windows and door is still quite light. The interior is lit as if no electric light is on. (It gets darker as the Act progresses)*

Neville Smallwood, dressed in his cloak and flamboyant hat and carrying the long cricket bag, approaches the front door. His head-and-shoulders silhouette is seen in the frosted glass panel. He knocks on the door. And again

Celia appears on the landing, wearing the dressing-gown which Neville wore in Act I and carrying a hairbrush. She hurries down, brushing her hair as she goes, and opens the front door

Neville stands in the doorway. He is very nervous, which makes him even more gawky and nerdish than usual. He does, it has to be said, cut rather a bizarre figure in his cloak and hat

Celia Good-evening. You must be Mr Smallwood.
Neville Yes, I'm Celia Wallis and you're Neville Smallwood.
Celia I beg your pardon?
Neville Oh, I'm sorry. I got it all wrong. You see, I've spent so much time imagining what I would say to you when I met you face to face that I ... I'm terribly sorry.
Celia Don't worry. Do come in. My directions were all right?
Neville Oh yes. "Turn left down the lane by Lodge Cottage." No problem.

As you see — (*he shrugs awkwardly*) because here I am.

Celia I got caught on the phone. I'm not even properly dressed.

Neville You look very lovely to me. Don't put any clothes on on my account.

Neville comes into the room and Celia closes the door behind him, giving him a slightly old-fashioned look. Neville comes to the centre of the room, and looks around in a state of delighted bewilderment

Goodness, this place is huge. It's like a barn.

Celia Yes, well, it was a barn.

Neville Ah. That would explain it. Well, well, well. You've no idea how many times I've imagined this moment.

Celia What?

Neville Me, Neville Smallwood, actually being inside the home of you, Celia Wallis.

Celia Yes?

Neville I never dared imagine that it might actually happen ——

Celia Really?

Neville — and yet here it is, actually happening ...

Celia Right.

Neville (*with a strange little shudder of delight*) I feel as if I've died and gone to heaven.

Celia Well, do sit down, Mr Smallwood. And let me take your coat — your cloak.

Neville Oh, thank you. (*He realizes he's still got his hat on*) Dear, oh dear, tsk, tsk, bad mark for manners, Neville. Hat on indoors, and in the presence of a lady. Goodness, Mother'd give me a real ticking-off.

Celia Would she?

Neville Certainly would. Forgive me. (*He takes his hat off*) Yes, thank you, I would be most grateful if you could take my hat.

Celia (*taking the hat from Neville*) It's a rather splendid hat, isn't it?

Neville Do you recognize it?

Celia Should I?

Neville It's like the one your husband wears. I saw a photo of him in the paper once, wearing a hat like this, and I thought, "Well, if that's how Celia Wallis likes a man to look, then that's the headgear for me."

Celia Ah. Could I take your cloak too ... ?

Neville Oh yes. (*He takes his cloak off with a flamboyant swirl copied from some movie he must once have seen. The gesture doesn't quite work. The removal of the cloak reveals that Neville is dressed underneath in an ultra-conventional suit, shirt and tie*) Voilà!

Neville hands the cloak to Celia

Celia I must say you wear these with some style.

Neville Oh yes. I'm quite a well-known figure on the South Coast.

Celia So I've heard.

Neville Some of us are always going to rise above the conventional, aren't we? Some of us are always going to be free spirits.

Celia (*putting the cloak and hat on a chair*) Undoubtedly.

Neville Of course, I don't need to tell you that, do I, what with you being an actress and all. Bohemia's your natural habitat, eh?

Celia Maybe. Please sit.

Neville (*sitting on the sofa*) Thank you very much.

Celia And just excuse me for a moment, while I go and get changed.

Neville Of course. (*He looks at his watch*) I'm sorry. Was I early?

Celia No. (*She heads for the stairs*) I got caught on the phone, that's all.

Neville Ah.

Celia (*moving up the stairs*) Do, please, make yourself at home while I … (*She listens to the following with disbelief*)

Neville Slip into something comfortable … ? Though, actually, that's wrong. Normally people say that line when they're going to slip out of a dress into a négligé, whereas you're already in a négligé and are slipping into a dress, which is, er … (*He lets out a strange little giggle*)

Celia gives a bemused look at Neville over the banister, and goes off down the passage to her bedroom

Left on his own downstairs, Neville can hardly contain his excitement and curiosity at actually being in his idol's home. He sits for a moment, but can't stay still. He goes across to the Henry VIII dummy and investigates it, managing to knock its head off. He replaces this and goes to peer through the glass doors of Martin's study. Then, to his great delight, he sees the "Annie Get Your Gun" rifle, knife and ammunition belt on their mountings. The rifle exercises a strong magnetism for him. He cannot stop himself from reaching up to take it down from the wall. He looks at the rifle in his hands with reverence bordering on idolatry

Celia appears on the landing. She is wearing the costume she wore in Act I, and looks very good in it

Celia Is that a gun or are you just pleased to see me?

Neville (*not getting the reference; in confusion*) Of course I'm pleased to see you. (*He fumbles to return the rifle to its mounting*) I'm sorry. I shouldn't have touched it. I ——

Celia (*heading down the stairs*) Don't worry.

Neville (*turning round to look at Celia*) That's a lovely dress.

Celia Thank you.

Neville I've never seen one like that before. Mother doesn't wear that kind of thing.

Celia I should hope not.

Neville (*indicating the display of memorabilia*) Sorry about the rifle. I must say you have a magnificent array of memorabilia. Almost like a shrine.

Celia It is a shrine. A shrine to Martin Powell. Trouble is it only has one worshipper — and that's Mártin Powell.

Neville (*pointing to the Golden Heart*) What's that one?

Celia It's his "Variety Club Award".

Neville What for?

Celia Biggest Ego in the Business.

Neville Is it really?

Celia No, of course it isn't. It was "Best Actor in a Revival". For his Richard III. Now can I get you a drink? Coffee? Tea? Or maybe something stronger ... ?

Neville No. No, thank you. Certainly not something stronger when I've got work to do. I'm not a great drinker, actually.

Celia Oh.

Neville No. I mean, I'm not a total abstainer. (*A little roguishly*) Mother and I have been known to hit the sherry at Christmas.

Celia But you're not the stereotype of the hard-drinking journalist.

Neville No, by no means, no.

Celia Well, what about tea or coffee?

Neville Oh yes, I do drink them.

Celia Which?

Neville Sorry?

Celia Which would you like? Tea or coffee?

Neville I see what you mean. No, I meant I do drink them, but I won't have either at the moment, thank you very much.

Celia Right.

Neville But don't let me inhibit you if you fancy a quick noggin.

Celia (*looking at him slightly curiously*) No. I'll have a "quick noggin" after we've done the interview.

Neville Yes. Which is of course why I am here, isn't it?

Celia Yes.

Neville (*suddenly alarmed*) Do you think I should be getting on with it, the interview? I mean, you may be pressed for time, and here's me wittering away ...

Celia I'm not pressed for time.

Neville Oh, good. (*Confidentially*) As a matter of fact, I haven't done a lot of interviews, you know.

Celia Really?

Neville Not radio ones, that is. I've done lots of newspapers. Local newspapers, mind. But radio interviews are different.

Celia Yes, they are.

Neville Mm.

Celia For one thing, your voice gets heard.

Neville What?

Celia Your voice gets heard. There's a real possibility that the listeners might hear your voice.

Neville Yes, right. (*As if the idea's never occurred to him*) That's a thought, isn't it?

Celia Have you *ever* done a radio interview before?

Neville Oh yes. Only for a local station, though. Do you know Radio Two Towns?

Celia No, I don't.

Neville Well, it's a smallish station ...

Celia Just serving the two towns, eh?

Neville You do know it.

Celia There was a clue in the name.

Neville Oh yes. Yes, of course. (*He gives another odd little giggle*) They were going to give me my own regular slot. (*He goes into an inept impression of a radio presenter*) "And now it's over to our Showbiz Correspondent, Neville Smallwood ... " (*Back in his own voice*) But, er, nothing came of it.

Celia Budgets are always tight in local radio. Did they run out of money?

Neville Oh, they weren't paying me.

Celia (*fetching a vase from Martin's study*) Ah. (*Somewhat surprised*) So you're quite lucky that Radio Two have agreed to broadcast this interview ... I mean, given your — if you don't mind my saying it — limited experience.

Neville I think the only reason they're using me is because I'm the one who's got you to agree to do an interview.

Celia Perhaps.

Neville (*with another of his funny little chuckles*) Actually, the producer said if I'm too dreadful, they can always cut out my questions and just use your answers. (*Modestly*) It is you the listeners really want to hear from, not me.

Celia I suppose so.

Neville Not that I plan being dreadful, let me tell you. Oh no, I've done a lot of preparation. This is going to be my breakthrough into national broadcasting. I do know my showbiz.

Celia So I gathered from your letter.

Neville And everyone in — (*he uses the phrase rather self-consciously*) "the business" started from nowhere, didn't they?

Celia I know I did.

Neville (*slyly*) I know exactly where you started. Straight out of RADA to play Annie Oakley in *Annie Get Your Gun* at the Haymarket Theatre, Leicester. I can tell you the exact date.

Celia I'm sure you can. (*Slightly coyly*) But I don't think we need to tell the listeners that, do we?

Neville (*not understanding her meaning*) Why not?

Celia (*moving towards the kitchen with the vase*) Well, some of them can probably count.

Celia exits into the kitchen

Neville (*still not understanding*) Oh, right. Whatever you say. I think you'll find I know quite a lot about your career.

Celia (*off*) I gathered that from your letter too.

Neville Oh yes. I saw you in that *Annie Get Your Gun*. First thing I saw you in.

Celia enters with the vase full of water

It would have been hard to see me in anything before. That was my first job.

Neville I know. I thought you made a wonderful Annie Oakley.

Celia (*putting the flowers in the vase*) Thank you.

Neville She's a magnificently strong character, isn't she?

Celia Yes.

Neville Even so, her life's not all plain sailing. She has her moments of heartbreak.

Celia Mm.

Neville No, I said to Mother after we saw you in the show the first time, "That's the sort of woman I want."

Celia (*slightly alarmed*) What do you mean:"want"?

Neville Well, I mean if ever I was so fortunate as to marry, you are exactly the sort of woman I would like to be my bride.

Celia Ah.

Neville No, not the *sort* of woman. *The* woman. The only woman.

Celia Mm.

Neville Which is why of course I've never married ...

Celia (*even more alarmed*) Oh.

Neville Well, you having married Martin Powell made it a bit difficult for me, didn't it? (*He does his unnerving little chuckle again*) He's rather in the way, so far as any plans I might have in that direction are concerned, eh?

Celia Look, I'm sorry if I've blighted your life.

Neville (*thoughtfully*) Yes, you have blighted it, actually. And I would be very angry about your having blighted it ——

Celia (*apprehensively*) Oh?

Neville — were it not for the fact that you have also enriched it so much. No, no, on balance the enrichment has been far greater, immeasurably greater, than any blighting that might inadvertently have occurred.

Celia Good. (*Still rather ill at ease*) You spoke of the "first" time you saw *Annie Get Your Gun*. How many times did you see it?

Neville (*proudly*) Mother and I went nine times.

Celia But it was only a four-week run.

Neville Oh yes. But when I get keen on something, I get keen on it. I'm not fickle. I don't get diverted.

Celia (*with mounting unease*) Maybe we should get on with the interview?

Neville Yes, absolutely, so we should. That is, after all, what I'm here for, isn't it?

Celia Yes.

Neville (*going across to his bag*) I've got all my own gear, you know. I bought it. Investing for the future of my career. (*He produces a cassette recorder and puts it on the coffee table*) This is very good. Excellent sound quality. It's got an integral microphone, but — (*he produces a large telescopic mike stand*) I thought you might feel more at ease with an external mike on a stand.

Celia I think quite honestly I'd feel more at ease if we just put the cassette player on the table and do it here.

Neville (*rather taken aback*) Dear oh dear. When I rehearsed the interview with Mother, we did it standing up with a mike on a stand.

Celia (*amazed*) You actually rehearsed the whole interview with your mother?

Neville (*proudly*) Oh yes. I didn't want to be accused of coming here badly prepared.

Celia (*weakly*) No ...

Neville (*with another little chuckle*) Mind you, I'm expecting you to give more interesting answers than Mother did.

Celia Thank you.

Neville I mean, Mother's a wonderful woman, absolutely fascinated by showbiz, but, er, she's not part of it in the way you are. And, actually, her life's probably been less interesting than yours has.

Celia If you say so.

Neville She worked for the Post Office in Leicester for forty-four years, and then retired to Rustington-on-Sea. Not a lot of meat there for an interview, really, is there?

Celia Perhaps not.

Neville So you think we'd be all right just sitting with the recorder on the table?

Celia Yes. We'll be more relaxed.

Neville (*not totally convinced by this*) Ah.

Celia Are you trying to say that you think we're a bit far away from the microphone?

Neville nods embarrassedly

Well, why don't you join me? Unless, of course, you'd rather not sit on the sofa with me?

Neville (*very excitedly*) Oh, good heavens, I've *dreamt* of sitting on the sofa with you. Lots of nights I've gone to sleep with my mind absolutely full of the idea of … (*he recovers himself*) No, no, that'll be fine. (*He sits beside her on the sofa; awkwardly*) Right, well maybe we should start?

Celia Yes.

Neville (*reaching into his pocket and producing some rather scruffy A4 sheets covered with hand-written notes*) Just get all my notes together.

Celia (*springing up from the sofa with some relief*) Oh, you probably haven't got enough light to read. (*She moves to a lamp*)

Neville No, I'm fine.

Celia switches a lamp on, and returns to the sofa. Neville looks embarrassed as she comes and sits close beside him again. She quite enjoys his embarrassment

Celia There.

Neville Right. Yes. (*He straightens up the cassette player on the table and turns to face Celia*) So … (*in an inept cod-American accent*) let's get this show on the road. Celia Wallis ——

Celia Aren't you going to put a tape in?

Neville What? Oh, yes. (*He rummages in the bag and produces a cassette tape, which he puts into the cassette player*) Special long-playing tape this is. Do you know, it can record up to three hours.

Celia (*appalled at the prospect*) And how long is the interview supposed to be?

Neville Five minutes.

Celia Well, we should be just about covered, shouldn't we?

Neville Yes. (*He opens his mouth as if he's about to start the interview*)

Celia What about level?

Neville Oh, not too intellectual. It is Radio Two, after all.

Celia No, I meant sound level. Usually the interviewer asks some question like: "What did you have for breakfast?"

Neville (*looking straight at Celia*) Celia Wallis, what did you have for breakfast?

Celia I had a plain yoghurt, half a grapefruit and one slice of toast.

Neville (*still looking at her*) I see.

Celia You hadn't got it switched on.

Neville What? Er, no. (*He switches on the recorder and presses the "play"
and "record" buttons*) Mm, that's recording. Little red light goes on when
it's recording. Well, it blinks, actually. Celia Wallis, what did you have for
breakfast?

Celia I had a twenty-four-ounce steak, with French fries, hash browns, black
pudding and a toffee fudge sundae.

Neville (*looking at her in surprise*) Did you? (*He presses the "stop" button
on the tape*)

Celia No, of course I didn't. That was a joke.

Neville Ah. (*He presses the "rewind" button on the cassette player*) I have
dried apricots. Every morning. Mother's always been a great one for dried
apricots. (*He indicates that the tape has rewound*) Ah, there we are. (*He
presses the "play" button*)

The tape recorder plays; once it has started, they talk over it

Neville's Voice Celia Wallis, what did you have for breakfast?

Celia's Voice I had a twenty-four-ounce steak, with French fries, hash browns, black pudding and a toffee fudge sundae. **Neville's Voice** Did you?	**Celia** Sounds fine. Shall we start? **Neville** Yes. Perhaps I should just wind the tape back. **Celia** You've got three hours. It's not going to run out. **Neville** No, no, but ... (*he stops the tape and presses the "rewind" button*)

I just don't want the opening to sound untidy, unprofessional; you know,
for the producer.

Celia Right. And you say the interview's actually going out in tonight's
programme?

Neville Yes. The BBC said they'd arrange a courier to collect the tape.

Celia All fixed. They rang for directions. They're coming at nine forty-five.

Neville And the courier's also going to take some publicity stuff which your
agent said you had ... ?

Celia Packed up and ready to go.

Neville Good. The interview'll go out just before midnight. So they'll have
time to edit the tape if necessary. And if they think it's really unbroadcastable,
they've got a feature on morris dancing they can slot in instead.

Celia What?

*The cassette's reset. Neville turns purposefully to Celia. He asks his
questions from his sheets of notes*

Neville (*reading*) Celia Wallis, your career started in musicals. Straight out
of drama school you went to play the lead in *Annie Get Your Gun* at the
Haymarket Theatre, Leicester, but subsequently diversified more into
straight drama, the highspots of your career to date perhaps being Vittoria
in *The White Devil* at Chichester and, for the Royal Shakespeare Company,
your Lady Macbeth in the play of that name — that is *Macbeth*, not "Lady
Macbeth" — not to mention many very fine television performances on
television, notably Kate in the Granada Television series "Partnership".
Do you ever wish that you had continued to concentrate on the musicals?

Celia No.

Neville (*thrown by the brevity of Celia's response*) Oh. Oh dear. Mother
actually gave a rather fuller reply when I asked her that.

Celia (*not unkindly*) Maybe you did give a little too much information in the
question. It might be better if you shortened it.

Neville Yes. Yes. Right. (*He consults his notes*) Celia Wallis, your career
started straight out of drama school in a musical, *Annie Get Your Gun* in
fact. Do you ever wish that you had continued to concentrate on musicals?

Celia No. I'm the kind of actress whose main pleasure comes from getting
inside the skin of a character so totally that I actually lose my own identity
in the identity of the person I'm playing. And I find that's a lot more
difficult to do in the unnaturalistic setting of a musical. I enjoy musicals a
lot — I've enjoyed all the ones I've been in — but the emphasis of my career
will always be in the theatre. That's my first love.

Neville I see. (*He consults his notebook*) So, Celia Wallis, if Andrew Lloyd
Webber offered you the starring role in his next musical, would you accept
it?

Celia I'd obviously be very flattered, but if there was a nice juicy dramatic
role around, I'd go for that rather than the musical.

Neville I see. The musical-lovers' gain would be the straight theatre's loss.

Celia (*working this out*) I beg your pardon?

Neville (*realizing what he's said*) Oh, I'm sorry. I meant "The straight
theatre's gain would be the musical-lovers' loss." (*Out of interview mode*)
Don't worry, the producer'll be able to edit that out.

Celia Good.

Neville (*going back into interview mode, consulting his notebook*) Celia
Wallis, do you have a favourite role that you would like to play but have
not yet played?

Celia Well, there are a couple. I'd love to play Rosalind in *As You Like It*.

Neville I see.

Celia I'm really too old for the part, but I think I could still just get away with
it.

Neville I see. (*He goes into inept complimentary mode*) Oh, I'm sure you
could get away with it, Celia Wallis. You're extremely well-preserved.

Celia (*slightly miffed*) Thank you.

Neville You said there were two parts you'd like to play. What's the other one?

Celia Cleopatra. That's my absolutely favourite part. (*Helpfully*) *Antony and Cleopatra.*

Neville Right. In the play of the same name. (*He consults his notes*)

Celia once again looks at him curiously

Celia Wallis, you are currently rehearsing a new play called "The Horse Doctor", which is due to open at the Theatre Royal in Brighton next week; but do you have any plans for the future?

Celia I'm full of plans for the future. There are so many exciting projects in the air at the moment that I can't decide between them. Still, (*she reaches to put her hand on Neville's knee*) that's a wonderful problem for an actress to have.

Celia touches Neville. At the contact of her hand, Neville jumps like a scalded cat. He knocks over the vase of flowers on the coffee table. Flowers and water go everywhere

(*Too late*) Aaah!

Neville (*leaping to his feet*) Oh, no! I'm so sorry. (*He moves quickly to rescue the cassette recorder, putting it on the side table with his notes on top of it*)

Celia (*taking control*) Don't worry. It's only water.

Neville Yes, but I feel so clumsy. Look, I'll mop it up.

Celia (*picking up the flowers and the vase*) It's no problem. (*She heads for the kitchen*) I'll just fill it up again.

Celia goes off into the kitchen

Neville (*rather awkwardly trailing across towards the kitchen door*) I am sorry. I think it's because I was nervous ——

Celia (*off*) Don't give it another thought.

Neville (*to himself, furiously*) You are such an idiot, Neville. So inept. We can't take you anywhere.

Celia enters with the vase refilled and carrying a cloth

Celia Look, it's sorted. No problem. (*During the following, she mops up the tabletop, quickly and efficiently, and moves to replace the vase of flowers there. Looking at Neville, she thinks better of this, and puts them on the mantelpiece*)

Neville What about the carpet?

Celia It's only water. That rug's seen much worse. In fact, if you wrung everything out of it, you could probably set up as a wine merchant.

Neville (*not quite getting the joke*) Ah. (*He gets it and gives a token chuckle*) Ah. Yes. Mm. (*Then, anxiously*) And you really did think the interview went all right?

Celia It was fine.

Neville (*relieved*) Good. The producer was very keen that I should use your name a lot, so that listeners who tuned in half-way through would know who I was talking to.

Celia I think you can rest assured that they'll be able to do that.

Neville (*anxiously*) I didn't get a twang, did I?

Celia I beg your pardon?

Neville Mother says that sometimes, when I get nervous, a twang creeps into my voice. Sort of Midlandsish, a rather common twang.

Celia I wasn't aware of any twang.

Neville No, good. (*Awkwardly*) I suppose I'd better be on my way ...

Celia There's no rush.

Neville No? Are you sure?

Celia Sure.

Neville (*looking around with some satisfaction*) Well, fancy me, Neville Smallwood, being here sitting on a sofa with you, Celia Wallis.

Celia (*springing up rather uneasily from the sofa*) Fancy. I certainly need a drink after that. Surely I can tempt you ... ?

Neville Well, maybe ...

Celia (*heading for the kitchen*) A little celebration of your first interview on national radio.

Celia exits into the kitchen

Neville (*packing up his tripod*) Yes. A good job jobbed. (*He calls out*) That's what Mother always says. "A good job jobbed."

Celia (*off; calling*) Does she?

Neville Oh yes. (*He relaxes even more and looks around him with increasing satisfaction*) Oh yes. She certainly does.

Celia enters from the kitchen, carrying a cold bottle of champagne

(*Uneasily*) Ooh, I say. Champagne.

Celia Don't you like it?

Neville I haven't had it that often.

Celia Oh.

Neville Just the once, actually. At a wedding. A friend of Mother's was getting married. I'm afraid I got a bit tiddley and misbehaved.

Celia Misbehaved?

Neville Well, got a bit raucous and rough.

Celia Rough?

Neville I hit him! I sort of lost my temper and hit someone. It was ... Mother had to give me quite a talking-to when we got home.

Celia What, was this when you were in your teens?

Neville No, no, just a couple of years ago.

Celia Ah. Is your father still alive?

Neville (*rather prickly*) I wouldn't know.

Celia Oh?

Neville He walked out on Mother when I was eighteen months old. Walked out on me too. We don't know where he is — and we don't care!

Celia (*handing him the bottle of champagne*) You open this and I'll get some glasses.

Neville Ooh, it's cold.

Celia It's been in the fridge. (*She goes to the cupboard above the drinks tray to get out two champagne flutes. She polishes them with her back to the audience*)

Neville has clearly never opened a champagne bottle before. He tries to unscrew the top

Neville I'm sorry if you thought my interview was a bit superficial, Miss Wallis.

Celia (*with her back to him*) Please don't call me "Miss Wallis". I'm Celia and you're Neville.

Neville (*very touched by the honour*) Ooh. Thank you — Celia. I was a bit worried that the interview could have been done by just anyone.

Celia How do you mean?

Neville Well, I probably know more about your career than any living human being ——

Celia Ah.

Neville — but somebody who didn't know anything about you could have asked the same questions. Still, the producer did say, keep it general, don't go into too much detail.

Celia (*putting the two glasses down on the table in front of the sofa*) So you were just fulfilling your brief. (*She takes the champagne bottle from him*) I'll do that.

Neville Yes. "Just fulfilling my brief."

Celia deftly opens the champagne and fills the two glasses during the following

I've got a huge collection of souvenirs and cuttings about you, you know.

Celia So you said on the phone. (*She holds out a glass of champagne to Neville*) Here you are.

Neville (*not taking the glass*) Well ... I wouldn't want to ...

Celia To what?

Neville To misbehave.

Celia Neville, you have my word for it — I will not allow you to misbehave.

Neville takes the glass

(*Raising her glass to Neville*) Cheers.

Neville (*raising his glass to Celia*) Down the hatch. (*He takes a big, clumsy swallow of champagne*) Ooh, it is bubbly.

Celia Yes, it is. That's why it's called "bubbly".

Neville Really? Never thought of that. (*He takes another big swallow of champagne*)

Celia You were talking about your collection of souvenirs. When did you start getting it together?

Neville Straight after I saw *Annie Get Your Gun* for the first time. That was the defining moment in my life, you know. Like St Paul on the road to Damascus.

Celia (*slightly uncomfortable*) Ah. Mind you, you wrote rather different epistles, didn't you?

Neville looks at her in puzzlement

Different from Paul's.

Neville still doesn't get the reference

So what kind of items have you got — you know, in your collection?

Neville Oh, some of it you wouldn't believe. I bet there's stuff you've forgotten you ever had. Clothes, all that kind of thing.

Celia (*a bit worried*) Clothes? You mean costumes, don't you? Not my personal clothes?

Neville Oh, no, no. Costumes from shows you were in.

Celia looks relieved

I have brought it all with me, you know.

Celia With you? What?

Neville My Celia Wallis collection. It's all in the car.

Celia Really?

Neville You did ask me to bring it.

Celia Did I? I don't remember.

Neville (*rather hurt*) Yes, you did. When we spoke on the phone, I said, "I've got this great collection of Celia Wallis memorabilia", and you said you'd be interested to see it.

Celia One day. I meant I'd be interested to see it one day. Not today specifically.

Neville (*crestfallen*) Oh, I'm sorry about that.

Celia Of course I'd be interested to see it today.

Neville (*excitedly gulping down the remains of his champagne*) There's one thing I've got that you just won't believe. (*He rises from the sofa and hurries to the front door*) It's nearly twenty years since you've seen it! Won't be a mo!

Neville hurries out of the front door and closes it behind him

Celia looks thoughtful, then refills Neville's champagne glass. She rises from the sofa and goes across to the wall where the "Annie Get Your Gun" rifle is displayed on its mounting. She looks at the rifle for a moment, then takes it down. She weighs it in her hands, raises it and sights along the barrel. She smiles enigmatically, perhaps caught up in the nostalgia of the moment. She goes into a subdued, pensive version, almost to herself, of the opening of "Anything You Can Do ..." from "Annie Get Your Gun". She is thoughtful for a moment, then replaces the rifle in its mounting

Neville comes hurrying in, carrying the life-size cut-out of the twenty-two-year-old Celia Wallis in "Annie Get Your Gun" hat and costume. He stands it up

Celia Good heavens.

Neville Surprise, surprise, eh? I bet you never thought you'd see this again.

Celia That is certainly true. (*She looks at the cut-out rather poignantly*) It's a cruelty unique to my profession ... the way one is constantly presented with images of one's younger self. The mirror in the morning's bad enough. Something like this just rubs salt in the wound.

Neville Don't worry. You still look wonderful. You'll always be wonderful to me, you know, Celia.

Celia Ah.

Neville Even when you're dead.

Celia (*with a little shudder*) Oh. (*She hastily hands him his refilled champagne glass*) Here you are. Drink up.

Neville Ooh. (*He takes a substantial swallow*)

Celia (*moving to the rifle mounted on the wall*) You're quite interested in this, aren't you, Neville?

Neville Yes, I'm sorry. I shouldn't have touched it, but ... It's wonderful. It brings it all back: *Annie Get Your Gun*; the first time I saw you.

Celia The producer presented it to me at the end of the run. A little thank-you for ... everything. It's been mounted up there since we bought this place ... but I have no sentimental feelings for it.

Neville It's a very precious memento.

Celia Not for me, it isn't. Any memories it carries are not of a triumphant stage production, just of the death of a marriage.

Neville doesn't seem to take in what she's saying. He is mesmerized by the sight of the rifle. It's all he can do to keep his hands off it

(*After a pause*) Would you like it?

Neville What? Oh, no, I couldn't. It's yours.

Celia I told you, it doesn't mean anything to me. (*She takes the rifle down from its mounting*) Go on, you have it.

Neville But I ——

Celia (*thrusting the rifle towards him*) There. It's yours. Really.

Celia hands Neville the rifle, then takes down the ammunition belt and hands it across

You'd better have this too. (*She turns back to the wall*) And my Annie Oakley knife too, I suppose. That was part of the costume too.

But Neville is too interested in the gun to think about the knife. He holds the gun reverentially

Neville Yes, yes. In a minute.

Celia leaves the knife where it is

Oh, Celia, I ... You've no idea what this means to me. Ooh, you just wait till I show Mother. She'll be over the moon.

Celia You don't have to handle it like bone china. It's quite robust. Lasted all those performances of *Annie Get Your Gun*.

Neville Yes. (*He takes the rifle more firmly into his hands. Then he raises the butt to his shoulder, and sights along the barrel*)

Celia watches Neville uneasily. Neville takes the rifle in a wide arc around the room, until it points at her

It's beautiful.

Celia What are you going to do with it?

Neville Well, there's only one thing I can do with it.

Celia (*nervously*) What?

Neville (*excitedly*) This. (*After a moment's pause, he goes straight into "You Can't Get A Man With A Gun" from "Annie Get You Gun". He does a full routine, with long-remembered choreography. As in Act I, there is something slightly inept and disturbing about the way he performs the song. Halfway through the second verse, carried away by the excitement of the moment, Neville pulls the trigger of the rifle, which fires. It hits Martin Powell's Golden Heart Variety Club Award, which shatters in its niche. Appalled*) Oh no! My God, what've I done?

Celia (*amused by what's happened*) You've converted "Best Actor in a Revival" to "Best Actor in a Smash".

Neville (*shocked*) It was a live bullet! You didn't use live bullets on stage, did you?

Celia No. The only time we ever used live ammunition was — for some charity …

Neville At the rifle range in Leicester.

Celia (*piecing the story together*) Right. Which would have been the last time I used the gun. (*Surprised*) The bullet must have been in there for all those years.

Neville (*looking despairingly at the debris*) Oh, but look at the mess I've made.

Celia (*moving towards the kitchen*) Don't worry about it.

Celia exits into the kitchen

Neville (*moving to follow Celia but not leaving the stage*) I'm such a clumsy idiot. First the flowers, now this …

Celia emerges from the kitchen with a dustpan and brush

Aren't you angry with me?

Celia (*sweeping up the debris*) I'm not angry with you. It's not my award. Martin may feel differently, though. You know what you've done to him … ?

Neville What?

Celia (*with a giggle*) You've broken his heart.

Neville (*vindictively*) Good.

Celia looks at him quizzically

I like the idea of Martin Powell being upset. After the way he's treated you.

Celia Oh, goodness. Are you going to be my knight in shining armour? To protect me from the evil dragon?

Neville I'd like to be. Seriously. I'd kill anyone who hurt you.

Celia (*lightly*) Thanks. But don't worry. So far as Martin's concerned, I can look after myself. (*She finishes sweeping up the debris, looks at the empty niche and then puts the vase of flowers from the mantelpiece into it. She moves towards the kitchen*) There, all done.

Celia exits into the kitchen

Neville looks at the rifle on the sofa, picks up the ammunition belt, and is thoughtful. We hear Celia returning from the kitchen. Neville hears Celia, puts the belt down, and moves away from the sofa

Celia enters

Celia Come on, sit down. You deserve another drink after that. (*She again tops up Neville's champagne glass*)

During the ensuing dialogue, Celia is bright and almost flirtatious, but also a bit wary. She's recognized that Neville's odd, but hasn't yet made up her mind quite how odd he is

Neville I have to say, I'm still amazed to actually be here.

Celia Well, you are here. You see, everything's possible.

Neville Yes. But I mean, me — Neville Smallwood — sitting here drinking champagne with Celia Wallis … Well …

Celia If my friends could see me now, eh?

Neville Mm. (*A pause*) Actually, I don't have that many friends.

Celia Oh.

Neville But Mother will be very impressed when I tell her.

Celia Good.

Neville (*after a pause*) You know all those letters I wrote you … ?

Celia I could hardly miss them, could I? There have been a good few.

Neville Yes. I suppose you get quite a lot of fan mail.

Celia Quite a lot, mm.

Neville Those fan letters I wrote you, I signed them.

Celia I know. I can read.

Neville Yes, but what I mean is … (*he is unsure whether or not to make the confession, and then decides "what the hell"*) I sent you a lot of other letters I didn't sign. Typewritten letters.

Celia (*slightly apprehensively*) Ah.

Neville Do you know the ones I'm talking about?

Celia I think I probably do, yes.

Neville Because those letters, the unsigned ones, those say what I really feel about you.

Celia (*elaborately casual*) Well, I suppose it's flattering, in a way.

Neville I mean, I know you'd never look at me as a ... You know, as a ... In a relationship kind of way ...

Celia (*uneasily*) I hardly know you, Neville — what sort of person you really are.

Neville But I do mean what I wrote in those letters. You are the lodestone of my life. I will always be there for you.

Celia Thanks.

Neville If you need anything done for you. If there's anyone who's bothering you, I'll always be ready to protect you. Whatever it involves.

Celia That'll be a great comfort for me to know, Neville.

Neville And in death you will be mine.

Celia can hardly stop herself from shuddering at this

It's very important to me that I'm part of your life.

Celia (*trying to defuse the potential seriousness of this*) You are. We're friends, aren't we?

Neville (*slowly*) Yes. Friends.

Celia Let's drink a toast. (*She tops up their glasses, emptying the bottle*) To two good friends. To you and me: Celia and Neville.

Neville Celia and Neville.

They clink glasses

The front door opens, to admit Martin Powell. He is a successful and charismatic actor, some ten years older than his wife. His manner is cynical and world-weary. He wears an expensive raincoat and a broad floppy hat. He looks with distaste at the couple on the sofa, then switches on the main lights

Celia and Neville turn towards Martin. Neville rises from the sofa in alarm

Martin Oh, my God. I knew you were into cradle-snatching, Celia, but this looks more like embryo research. (*He closes the front door behind him. He takes off his hat and raincoat and hangs them on the row of pegs by the front door*) I've become accustomed to your compulsive infidelity, darling, but I'm surprised you're reduced to this.

Celia This is Neville Smallwood.

Martin (*sarcastically*) Not *the* Neville Smallwood? I'm really honoured to meet you.

Neville It's not the way it looks. I'm not Celia's lover.

Martin I didn't for a moment think you were. My wife's never had the best of taste, but even she draws the line somewhere. And it tends to be marginally above the level of pond life. I'm Martin Powell, by the way, but I think you'd probably pieced that together.

Neville Yes. Obviously I've seen photographs of you. I've seen you on stage too, come to that.

Martin Well, aren't you the lucky one? Nice to know that a little genuine theatrical magic has illuminated your drab life. (*He sees the bottle on the table*) Champagne, eh? Am I allowed some? Or would that spoil the tête-a-tête?

Celia (*picking up the empty bottle*) There's none left in this one. I'll open another if you ——

Martin Don't put yourself to any trouble ... darling. I'm quite capable of opening my own champagne in my own house, thank you very much. (*He looks at the cut-out from "Annie Get Your Gun" for the first time*) Well, well, well, what have we here?

Neville It's mine. It's a publicity thing from ... (*He slightly stumbles over the title*) "Granny Ate Your Gun". (*He corrects himself*) Annie Get Your Gun. It's Celia in her first ——

Martin Yes, I do recognize her. Not that I saw the production. Before I made my wife's acquaintance, you know, that was. While I still had some hopes for happiness in my life. (*He looks closely at the cut-out, then at Celia*) God, Celia, you've aged. Perhaps you should take that cut-out along when you see the plastic surgeon — give him a kind of template, something to work back to. Mind you, it has captured your acting style perfectly. Your performances always tended to be rather cardboard, didn't they, darling?

Celia is unaffected by these insults; she has heard them all before. Neville however, is incensed

Neville How dare you say that about the most brilliant actress of her generation?

Martin (*looking at Neville*) This your new agent, is it, Celia?

Celia No. Neville is one of my fans.

Martin Oh, that puts him in a minority. Positively one of an endangered species these days. (*He looks closely at Neville*) Hmm ... In his eye I can see the demented gleam of the genuinely unhinged. Yes, he's one of your fans all right.

Neville I don't deny it. I'm Celia Wallis's greatest fan.

Martin I used to be quite impressed with her myself — till I got to know what she was really like.

Neville Look, don't you dare insult —— !

Martin (*forcefully and incisively*) Shut up! (*He indicates the cut-out*) Why don't you just take that ridiculous thing away?

Neville hesitates for a moment, as if he's about to come back with some line. But he can't think of anything. Sheepishly – and by now quite unsteadily – he picks up the cut-out and puts it under his arm. Martin picks up Neville's cloak and hat from the row of hooks and proffers them to Neville, handling them as if they were contaminated

Yours too, I assume. My wife's taste in clothes can be pretty erratic, but even she wouldn't be seen dead in these.

Neville (*defensively*) The hat's just like your hat.

Martin Yes. And a good hat emphasizes the personality of its wearer. Which is what mine does for me — and sadly also what yours does for you!

Martin throws the cloak at Neville, and slams the hat down on his head

(*Picking up Neville's cricket bag with the same fastidious distaste*) What is this?

Celia You can see. It's a bag.

Martin Takes one to know one, dear.

Neville (*furiously*) Now, listen, you ——

Martin (*chillingly authoritative*) No, you listen! (*He shoves the cricket bag at Neville*)

Neville takes the bag, clumsily because of all his other encumbrances

Take this. Take all your rubbish, and take yourself, out of my house!

Neville squares up to Martin. He tries to think of some riposte. Nothing comes

(*Opening the front door with a flourish*) Go on — out!

Neville tries to cross the room with dignity, which is quite difficult, given everything he's carrying. When he reaches the front door, he turns defiantly back to Martin, but the effect is spoiled by the fact that the "Annie Get Your Gun" cut-out bangs against the door as he turns. In exasperation, Neville stands the cut-out up on the doorstep

Neville (*muttering*) I'll take my stuff to the car.

Martin Good.

Celia You don't have to go, Neville.

Neville (*trying — and failing — to come up with a more powerful exit line*) Don't worry — I'll be back.

Martin (*drily*) Can hardly wait.

Clumsily, fumbling with his hat, cloak and cricket bag, but leaving the cut-out where it stands on the doorstep, Neville exits and closes the door behind him

In the ensuing scene, Celia does not rise to Martin's insults. She has heard them all before in the course of their tempestuous marriage

Martin So who is he?

Celia He came to do an interview with me for Radio Two.

Martin I thought you didn't do interviews.

Celia I made an exception.

Martin Yes, I gather that new show of yours needs all the publicity it can get.

Celia The play's very strong.

Martin That's what they said about the *Titanic*, sweetie. Bit of a comedown for you, though. Playing a minor role …

Celia It is not a minor role. It's a very important … (*She stops before the next word can comes out*)

Martin Ooh, I think we were about to hear the word "cameo", weren't we? Soon we'll have "rewarding" and "significant" and "telling", won't we? I do love all these euphemisms that start getting used when a career's on the slide.

Celia (*incensed*) My career is not on the slide!

Martin No? Been a while since you've had a major role on stage, though, hasn't it? And I heard they're not going to another series of the telly.

Celia Television planners have never had any taste.

Martin True. Otherwise, why would they have cast you in the first place?

Celia Martin … I have heard most of these insults before, you know. I'm not very interested in your tired old cracks.

Martin That's certainly mutual.

Celia (*stung by the insult, but deliberately not rising to it*) I thought the reason you'd come down this evening was for us to have a fairly civilized discussion about the next step in our relationship

Martin "The next step in our relationship." Goodness, doesn't that sound grand? Yes, all right, let's talk about it. (*He looks at his watch*) I haven't got long. Meeting Victoria at ten.

Celia Right.

Martin There's not much to say. I'm going to divorce you.

Celia On what grounds, as a matter of interest?

Martin That's not much of a problem these days. Adultery'll do, won't it?

Celia On whose side?

Martin Yours, obviously.

Celia What about you?

Martin *I've* been remarkably restrained ...

Celia Really?

Martin Well, obviously there were the Stage Door Jennies, but I always think it's very important that a creative artiste doesn't lose touch with ordinary people.

Celia I'm not going to bother rising to that.

Martin One can get so insular in show business. I get a great deal of feedback from meeting women from different walks of life. You'd be amazed the people who come to the theatre these days. Hairdressers, computer programmers ... Do you know, I even had a policewoman not that long ago?

Celia I'm not interested, Martin.

Martin No. You're right. None of them were very interesting. Victoria, though, is something else.

Celia I'll say.

Martin I'm going to marry Victoria.

Celia Yes. I'd worked that out some time ago.

Martin Because I love her. Because Victoria has given me what you never gave me. She's given me a part of herself. And I know I haven't got long ...

Celia What?

Martin Went to the quack for an MOT. He wasn't optimistic.

Celia What do you mean?

Martin The booze, the lifestyle, they've taken their toll ...

Celia I'm sorry.

Martin Don't pretend you care, Celia. The only thing of mine you've ever cared about is my money.

Celia That's not true. When we acted together, there was a real electricity.

Martin 'Fraid there's been a bit of a power failure since.

Celia At first, when we made love, it was wonderful ... but then you had a power failure there too, didn't you?

Martin (*incensed*) Our sex-life fell apart because you lost interest.

Celia No. Our sex-life fell apart because there were just the two of us. You could never give of your best without an audience, could you, Martin?

Martin I don't have any problems with Victoria. No, no, our sex-life is very exciting. Do you know the first thing I do when I get into bed with Victoria?

Celia Try to find her, I imagine.

Martin I just look at her in disbelief that any woman can be so sexy.

Celia Right now I'm sure she is. Using all her skills and lies to stimulate an elderly lover.

Martin Victoria makes me feel like a teenager.

Celia That's exactly what I said, Martin dear: "using all her skills and lies to stimulate an elderly lover". But once she's got a ring on her finger, she may find other interests — like spending your money.

Martin You mustn't judge everyone by your standards, Celia.

Celia I just think it's pathetic to see an old man being manipulated by a little gold-digger like that. (*Nostalgically*) You and I really had something, Martin. There were all those shows we planned to do together ... *Antony and Cleopatra* ... When I look back over our time together, do you know what I see?

Martin Your sell-by date ... ?

Celia is quite insulted

Incidentally, Celia, I'm going to see to it that you don't get a penny more of my money than is absolutely necessary.

Celia You'll have to make me some kind of divorce settlement.

Martin Yes. But it won't be a generous one. I do have a very good lawyer, you know. You're not going to be my widow "richly left". Victoria is.

Celia I see.

Martin Victoria offers me the chance of a little, late happiness. I'm going to seize that chance with both hands. And I'm going to leave you to manage on your own. Without my money. Or my contacts. You'll be just like any other actress of your age. Looks going, work hard to come by. (*He goes into an earnest, affected actress voice*) "The trouble is, nobody seems to write decent parts for women over a certain age." Even your Stalker will lose interest in you, Celia. No, Victoria and I will watch the meteoric decline of your career with interest ... and great pleasure.

Celia And you imagine that marrying Victoria is going to change you?

Martin Yes.

Celia It won't. You'll have a brief honeymoon period, then it'll fail ... like all your other relationships have failed. Still, there is a bright side. Presumably, once she's married, Victoria will stop working.

Martin She's a damn fine little actress.

Celia With the emphasis on the "little".

Martin (*knowing how much what he's saying will hurt Celia*) Victoria and I are going to do *Antony and Cleopatra* together.

Celia What's she playing — the asp?

Martin (*satisfied to have needled her at last*) I've an appointment with the solicitor tomorrow. And if you're fostering fond illusions of taking me through the courts, forget it. I've got chapter and verse on all your little lapses. It's merely a matter of how many names I choose to bring up in court — and whether or not I include tradesmen.

Celia You've got it all worked out.

Martin I've got it all worked out.

Celia If you think I'm going to give up my rights without a fight ——

Martin You don't have any rights.

Celia Yes, I do.

Neville enters. He is quite drunk now; the unaccustomed champagne has really got through to him. The "Annie Get Your Gun" cut-out is still where he left it, to one side of the doorstep

Martin You gave up all rights as a wife the minute you started behaving like a whore!

Neville Don't you dare call Celia a whore!

Martin Oh God, it's the "Fan Fatale". What are you doing back here?

Neville I came for my cassette recorder, but I never expected to hear anyone talking to his wife like that.

Martin Oh, didn't you? Well, I'll have you know, it's a husband's right to call his wife whatever he chooses. Particularly when he is speaking no more than the truth. Celia is a whore.

Neville You're just jealous because she's more talented than you are!

Martin (*turning on Neville; viciously*) Celia Wallis was nothing till she married me. And she had nothing until she married me. You see, young man, I was lucky enough to be born with the one thing every actor needs, if he's going to succeed.

Neville (*contemptuously*) Talent?

Martin Money. Private money. Which Celia has shown a miraculous skill in spending. But the money wasn't her only reason for marrying me. Oh no. She married me because I'd got something else she wanted. Contacts. You see, at the beginning of her career, Celia got all her work by sleeping with people ——

Neville I'm not listening to this.

Martin That's how she got the part in *Annie Get Your Gun* — she slept with the director.

Neville You're lying!

Celia Neville, don't worry about it. This is between us.

Neville No, it's not. It's bigger than that. This is about talent, God-given talent. (*He turns to Celia*) Your talent is not of this time, but of all time. It will shine like a beacon for ——

Martin Oh, for Christ's sake! You sound like a timeshare brochure. (*He turns away to the drinks tray. During the ensuing dialogue, he takes a whisky tumbler out of the cupboard and pours himself a large glass of whisky*)

Neville Don't you dare turn your back on me!

During the following, Neville picks up the rifle from the sofa. He takes a bullet from the ammunition belt and, with fumbling fingers, manages to break the rifle and load it. Celia watches with horrified fascination. Shaking considerably, Neville raises the rifle to his shoulder and points it at Martin's back. As Martin gets to the end of his speech, he turns with his drink to find himself looking down the barrel of a rifle

Martin (*with his back to Neville, casually*) Get stuffed. The talent of Celia Wallis is a very, very minor talent. She owes any success she has achieved to three things. One: she's pretty. Correction: she was pretty. Two: she's prepared to go to bed with people who might give her parts. Three — and, as I say, this is much the most important of the lot — she's married to me. But not for much longer. (*He turns and sees Neville with the rifle; unfazed*) Oh, my God. Who've we got here — Billy the Kid?

Neville (*his voice thick and slurred*) You take back what you said about Celia's talent.

Martin Or what? (*In a cod-cowboy accent*) You gonna tell me this town ain't big enough for the two of us? You gonna fill me fuller o' holes than a sieve?

Neville You take it back!

Martin No. I've never been one to take things back — particularly when they're true. (*He pushes the rifle away as if it was just a branch in his way and moves towards the study doors. He remembers something, reaches into his jacket pocket and produces a cassette tape*) Got some music I want to listen to, Celia dear. Specially commissioned for my next production. (*He puts the cassette into the stereo*) 'Tis Pity She's a Whore. Where the hell's my Golden Heart?

Celia It's being regilded.

The music starts. It is atmospheric, threatening, the start of the music which is heard at the beginning of Act I

Martin By the way, darling, did I mention that I rang the estate agents and put this place on the market this morning?

Celia No.

Martin Well, I did. I'll be keeping the London house, of course. And Victoria and I will buy somewhere else out of town. Brighton, we thought, possibly. Somewhere that isn't contaminated by unpleasant memories, anyway. Somewhere that has nothing to do with you. (*He smiles smugly, takes a long swallow from his drink, then turns and goes into the study. He switches on the desk lamp, sits behind the desk, and starts looking at a script*)

Neville, shaking even more, stays rooted to the spot. Then suddenly he raises the rifle to his shoulder again and advances jerkily to stand in the study doorway

Neville Y-Y-Y-You bastard!

Martin (*looking up; mildly*) Oh, do put that thing away. You're not going to shoot me.

Neville Aren't I? Aren't I?

Martin No, you're not. (*He returns to his script, calmly, almost contemptuously*)

Neville stands shaking for a long moment, with the rifle trained on his adversary. Then he sways, totters, and falls to the ground

Celia (*coming forward to help Neville*) Are you all right?
Neville I'm sorry. I feel ... It's the drink. I ...

Celia helps Neville to stand during the following

Celia Can you stand?
Neville I'm not used to ... I said ... You know, champagne, I ...
Celia Sit down. (*She manoeuvres him towards the sofa*) I'll get you some coffee.

Neville sways, dazed

Celia exits into the kitchen

Martin chuckles

Neville (*unsteadily*) Look, I'm all right. I ... Maybe I should go. (*He stumbles towards the front door, and opens it. The "Annie Get Your Gun" cut-out is still to one side. Neville grabs hold of it, as if to take it to the car, then sways uncomfortably. As he does so, he inadvertently (perhaps ... ?) manoeuvres the cut-out into position in the middle of the doorway. Then he remembers something*) Ooh, my cassette recorder. (*He staggers back into the room, closing the door behind him. He goes DS, and collapses against the back of the armchair*)

Celia comes back in from the kitchen, carrying a cup of coffee, and looks anxiously at Neville

Celia Drink this.
Neville (*slurring his words*) I don't want coffee — I feel so sleepy — I just want to lie down ...
Martin Oh, for God's sake, Celia!
Celia He can go to my room.

Celia puts down the coffee and helps Neville to get up and leads him towards the stairs

(*To Neville*) Can you manage the stairs?

Neville (*furiously*) Of course I can manage the stairs! (*He calms down*) Yes,
   I ... Yes, I — just need to sleep for a little ...

*During the following, Celia and Neville move up the stairs and on to the
landing*

Celia You'll soon feel better.
Neville (*his voice very slurred by now*) Sorry. First the interview, and then
   the flowers and ...
Celia Come on, Neville, I'll help you.

Celia leads Neville off from the landing

*Martin looks up at them, and lets out a triumphantly contemptuous laugh. He
walks confidently round the room to get himself a drink and sits on the sofa*

*Celia comes out on to the landing again. She stands there for a moment,
looking down at Martin, then switches off the landing light, comes downstairs
and crosses the sitting-room, heading for the kitchen*

   I'm just going to get myself another drink.

Celia exits into the kitchen

Martin Fine. Take advantage of my cellar while you can. Soon you're going
   to have to pay for your own drinks. That could be a nasty shock for someone
   with expensive tastes like yours. (*He switches off a lamp and goes into the
   study*) Have you ever even seen an electricity bill?

*Celia emerges from the kitchen, opening another bottle of champagne. She
goes across to the table in front of the sofa, and deliberately pours a little
champagne into the glass that Neville had. Then she picks up the phone and
dials a number*

   Who're you calling now?
Celia Gilly.

Martin grimaces. He obviously doesn't care for Gilly

   She's had some good news. It's all going well. Oh, it's engaged. (*She puts
   the phone down, picks up the champagne glass, then lifts up the rifle from
   the floor where Neville dropped it. She moves towards the study*)
Martin (*looking up at her approach*) Oh God, what is this? Are *you* planning
   to shoot me now?

Celia No. (*She moves through into the study, and proffers the rifle*) I thought you might want to shoot yourself.

Martin Why?

Celia When you've been in the depths of depression, you've often said ——

Martin But I'm not in the depths of depression.

Celia (*putting the champagne glass casually down on a shelf*) Even after what the doctor told you?

Martin Celia, I have never felt more cheerful in my life. You see, now I've got Victoria.

Celia (*coming back into the sitting-room*) Of course. It's the little things that count.

Martin (*following Celia into the sitting-room*) Sorry. Obviously it would be very handy for you if I did choose this evening to top myself. Then you'd still be my wife when I died, and cop the lot. But I've got rather beyond the stage of organizing my life for your convenience. In fact, I now try to arrange things so that they will cause you maximum *in*convenience.

Celia Charming.

Martin I've always had my charming side. No, Celia darling, if I ever did want to commit suicide, I would set the whole thing up to make it look like murder disguised as suicide. And I'd leave some pretty clear pointers to incriminate you.

Celia Thank you.

Martin (*with a smug grin*) Anything I can do to make your life as uncomfortable as possible, rest assured I'll do it.

Celia Great. (*She looks at her watch*) I must try Gilly again.

Martin Why?

Celia She's got the lead in *The Boy Friend*. I must congratulate her. Do you have to play that bloody muzak so loud?

Martin (*switching off the sitting-room lights*) Better than listening to you nattering away to that harpy. (*He returns to the study, closing the curtains but leaving them slightly open*)

Celia I'll call her from the kitchen. (*She heads for the kitchen*)

The only light source is the spill from the study, and the moonlight through the frosted panel in the front door. This reveals the silhouette of the head and shoulders of a man in a hat. As she is about to go through to the kitchen, Celia sees the silhouette. She lets out a gasp and stands still for a moment, paralysed with fear

Martin! Martin!

Martin (*appearing at the study doors*) What the hell is it?

Celia (*pointing to the front door*) There's someone there!

Martin Oh, for God's sake! (*He sends her up*) Go and phone Gilly. If I'm not back in ten minutes, call the police.

Celia backs off fearfully into the kitchen

Martin switches the sitting-room lights on again (thus blacking out the silhouette), crosses to the front door and opens it. Standing in the middle of the doorstep is the "Annie Get Your Gun" cut-out. Martin laughs and closes the front door

Celia emerges fearfully from the kitchen

Celia Who was it? Who was there?
Martin No-one.
Celia But I swear ——
Martin Oh, go and ring bloody Gilly!

Celia goes back into the kitchen

Martin switches off the sitting-room lights

The silhouette again becomes visible; this time it is, as yet unbeknownst to us, Inspector Bruton wearing Neville's hat and cloak

Martin goes through into his study, leaving the curtains slightly open, as before

The stage is empty and nearly dark. Only the spill from the study, and the watery moonlight behind the silhouette at the door shed any light on the scene. This tableau is held for a long time

Then suddenly the figure at the door moves. Bruton opens the door, and steps inside. He is carrying Neville's cricket bag; his face is hidden by the hat and his body outlines muffled by the cloak. In the minimal light onstage, the figure could conceivably be Neville or Celia ... or someone else. Bruton puts the cricket bag down on the bench below the row of pegs, moves to the sofa, and picks up the rifle. He then moves slowly towards the study, stands for a moment, immobile, outside, then gently pulls open the curtains, and slips inside. He closes the curtains behind him

(*As the curtains close*) What the hell are you —— ?

Martin's speech is cut short by the muffled sound of a rifle shot. He gives a cry of pain, which transforms into a liquid gurgle. There is a moment's silence. Then the cloaked and hatted figure slips quickly out of the study, puts the rifle into Neville's cricket bag and zips the bag closed, then switches off the music. The audience still cannot be certain who the figure is

The kitchen door opens, spilling light across the stage. Celia comes rushing onstage, ecstatic

Celia Scott! Darling! Did it work? Did it work, Scott? Is he dead?

The cloaked figure removes his hat with rubber-gloved hands, to reveal that he is — Inspector Bruton. But this is a new Inspector Bruton. The plodding detective of Act 1 has been replaced by a sexy, charismatic figure

Bruton I don't miss from that range. I wasn't expecting that bloody music. (*He removes the cloak and crosses to hang up the cloak and hat*) When you phoned me on the mobile — when I was waiting up by Lodge Cottage — and you said, "Everything's going well", was Martin in the room?
Celia Yes.
Bruton (*admiringly*) You're a cool one.
Celia (*with self-satisfaction*) I'm an actress. (*She has a moment of conscience*) You know, we owe a lot to Neville.
Bruton Yes. He was the perfect fall-guy. His previous conviction was just icing on the cake.

Celia gives Bruton the ammunition belt

Celia We've got a lot to thank him for.
Bruton If Neville hadn't sent you those letters, we'd never have met. (*He looks at Celia*) You're not going soft on me, are you? Remember, you've got a tough interrogation ahead of you.

Celia nods resolutely. She'll be OK

The champagne glass ... the one I drugged ... ?
Celia All safely washed up. What now?
Bruton You must have a look.
Celia I don't want to.
Bruton You have to. When I arrive to investigate the murder, you've got to describe exactly how you found him. And the more shocked you sound, the better.
Celia Yes, yes, of course. (*She steels herself and nods to him to open the doors*) OK.

Bruton flings the study doors open. Illuminated by the desk light is exactly the scene with which the play opened. Martin lies back in his chair, with blood from the wound in his forehead over his face and chest, and more blood spattered on the wall behind him. Bruton goes into the study and opens the curtains over the glass panels

Celia (*turning away*) All right. That's enough.
Bruton (*looking at his watch*) I must go.
Celia How long shall I wait before I call the police?
Bruton Do it straight away. Fisher'll take the call in the office. Then he'll get through to me on my mobile. And turn on that music. (*He moves to the front door*)
Celia Kiss me.

They go into a clinch, then draw apart

(*Remembering something*) The letter. The new Stalker's letter.

Bruton nods, takes the letter out of his pocket and puts it on the drinks table

Bruton (*with a grin*) See you shortly ... (*he goes into policeman self-parody*) Miss Wallis.

Bruton exits out of the front door

Celia closes the door behind him. She seems quite blithe and cheerful. She goes across to the sitting-room phone. She dials three digits. The phone is answered at the other end

Celia Yes, Police, please. (*She starts sobbing and generally doing a very convincing distraught-widow act*) Hallo? Hallo. Listen, my name's Celia Wallis, and — my husband's been murdered! I just came in and found his body. My husband's been murdered! He's covered in blood and ... Yes, it's Exton's Barn, off Lodge Lane. You know it? ... As soon as you can. Please! (*She puts the phone down. In an instant, she turns from distraught widow to triumphant conspirator*) Yeah! (*She raises her glass towards the study*) Cheers, Martin. Remember — nobody upstages Celia Wallis and gets away with it! (*She laughs and toasts him. Keeping her champagne glass, she switches on the music*)

Celia hurries off upstairs, almost skittish in her triumph

All the lights on the stage slowly dim down, until the only light source is a very tight pinpoint of blinking red light on the side table. It comes from Neville's cassette recorder, which hasn't been switched off, and is still recording ... The blinking red light pulses, as ——

The CURTAIN *falls*

FURNITURE AND PROPERTY LIST

With the exception of the properties marked *, and the champagne bottles, which must be identical but one empty, one full, the properties are the same in ACT II as in ACT I

ACT I

On stage: STUDY
Desk. *On it*: desk lamp, manuscript

SITTING-ROOM
Sofa
Armchairs
Coffee tables. *On one*: empty champagne bottle
Occasional tables. *On one*: cassette recorder (practical) covered with
    pages of notes
Drinks cupboard. *In it*: two champagne flutes (at least)
Drinks table. *On it*: drinks, glasses, letter
Desk. *On it*: papers, large labelled Jiffy bag containing biographical
    material and photographs of **Celia**, address book
Stereo unit
Telephone
Vase
Life-size dummy with complete Henry VIII costume
Framed posters and production photographs (including one of **Martin**
    as Richard III)
Citations and awards
Guns
Swords
Daggers
Sheathed knife
Vase of flowers
On a shelf: empty champagne flute
On pegs: cloak, raincoat, two hats
Long cricket bag. *In it*: Wild West-style rifle, Western-style leather
    ammunition belt, large, labelled Jiffy bag, stapler

Off stage: Torches (**Bruton, Fisher, Leach**)
Instrument cases (**Fisher**)
Practical spotlights (**Wilkins** and **Carter**)
Evidence bags (**Carter**)

Tissue **(Celia)**
Tissue **(Neville)**
Computer printout **(Leach)**
Tray with cups of coffee **(Celia)**
Life-size cut-out of younger **Celia** as Annie Oakley **(Stage Management)**

Personal: **Bruton**: rubber gloves, notebook, pen, mobile phone
Fisher: rubber gloves, notebook, pen
Neville: watch (worn throughout)
Celia: watch (worn throughout)
Martin: watch (worn throughout)

ACT II

Clean study wall
Close study doors

Re-set: Vase with flowers from Variety Club Award niche on mantelpiece
Vase on study desk
Sheath knife in niche
Two champagne flutes in cupboard above drinks tray

Set: Flowers on coffee table
Rifle and ammunition belt in niche
"Variety Club Award" in niche

Strike: Cloak, raincoat, hats
Spotlights, instrument cases

Off stage: Hairbrush **(Celia)***
Long cricket bag. *In it*: cassette recorder, cassette tape, telescopic microphone stand **(Neville)**
Cloth **(Celia)***
Bottle of champagne **(Celia)**
Life-size cut-out of younger **Celia** as Annie Oakley **(Neville)**
Cup of coffee **(Celia)***
Letter **(Bruton)**
Dustpan and brush **(Celia)**

Personal: **Neville**: A4 sheets of hand-written notes
Bruton: letter
Martin: cassette

LIGHTING PLOT

Practical fittings required: table lamps, desk lamp, spotlights (see Furniture and Property List)
Interior with exterior backing to doors and windows. The same throughout

ACT I

To open: Near-total darkness; faint moonlight effect on exterior backing, fading to black by p.30; covering red blinking pinpoint light on cassette player (if necessary; see Author's Note p. vi)

Cue 1	Sound of car approaching and parking *Beam of headlights sweeps across stage*	(Page 2)
Cue 2	Car noise stops *Cut headlights*	(Page 2)
Cue 3	Sound of second car approaching and parking *Beam of headlights sweep across stage, more slowly than in Cue 1; blue flashing light*	(Page 2)
Cue 4	Car noise stops *Cut headlights but retain flashing lights*	(Page 2)
Cue 5	**Celia** switches on landing light *Snap on landing light*	(Page 4)
Cue 6	**Fisher** switches on downstairs lights *Snap on sitting-room lights*	(Page 4)
Cue 7	Sound of car approaching and parking *Beam of headlights sweeps across stage*	(Page 5)
Cue 8	Car noise stops *Cut headlights*	(Page 5)
Cue 9	**Bruton** looks at champagne flute on shelf *Cut blue flashing lights*	(Page 6)
Cue 10	**Neville** presses "stop" button on cassette recorder *Cut blinking red light*	(Page 30)

Cue 11	**Neville** presses "rewind" button *Snap on blinking red light*	(Page 30)
Cue 12	**Neville** presses "stop" button *Cut blinking red light*	(Page 30)
Cue 13	**Carter** and **Wilkins** switch off the spotlights *Cut spotlights*	(Page 35)
Cue 14	**Celia** switches off the sitting-room lights *Cut sitting-room lights*	(Page 35)
Cue 15	Long silence; then, when ready *Bring up car headlights through front door*	(Page 36)
Cue 16	**Bruton** switches on the sitting-room lights *Snap on sitting-room lights; cut headlights*	(Page 36)

ACT II

To open: Quite bright light on exterior backing, fading to watery moonlight during scene; unobtrusive lighting in sitting-room to suggest natural light, not electric light

Cue 17	**Celia** switches on a lamp *Snap on practical lamp*	(Page 46)
Cue 18	**Neville** switches on the cassette recorder *Snap on blinking red light*	(Page 47)
Cue 19	**Neville** presses the "stop" button *Cut blinking red light*	(Page 47)
Cue 20	**Neville** presses the "rewind" button *Snap on blinking red light*	(Page 47)
Cue 21	**Neville** presses the "stop" button *Cut blinking red light*	(Page 47)
Cue 22	**Neville** presses the "rewind" button *Snap on blinking red light*	(Page 47)
Cue 23	**Martin** switches on the main lights *Snap on main lights*	(Page 57)
Cue 24	**Martin** switches on the study desk lamp *Snap on study table lamp*	(Page 64)

Cue 25	**Celia** switches off the landing light	(Page 66)
	Snap off landing light	
Cue 26	**Martin** switches off a lamp	(Page 66)
	Snap off practical lamp	
Cue 27	**Martin** switches off the sitting-room lights	(Page 67)
	Snap off sitting-room lights	
Cue 28	**Martin** switches on the sitting-room lights	(Page 68)
	Snap on sitting-room lights	
Cue 29	**Martin** switches off the sitting-room lights	(Page 68)
	Snap off sitting-room lights	
Cue 30	**Celia** hurries off upstairs	(Page 70)
	Fade all lights except blinking red light on cassette player	

EFFECTS PLOT

ACT I

Cue 1   As CURTAIN rises   (Page 2)
           Eerie, dramatic music on stereo

Cue 2   When ready   (Page 2)
           Sound of car approaching and stopping

Cue 3   Car headlights are switched off   (Page 2)
           Sound of second car approaching and stopping

Cue 4   **Fisher**'s torch beam finds **Martin**'s body   (Page 3)
           Dark chord in music

Cue 5   **Fisher** switches off the music   (Page 4)
           Cut music

Cue 6   **Celia**: "Thank you."   (Page 5)
           Sound of cars approaching and stopping

Cue 7   **Bruton**: "Now, Miss Wallis ——"   (Page 24)
           Mobile phone rings

Cue 8   **Neville** presses the "play" button   (Page 30)
           Taped dialogue as p. 30

Cue 9   **Neville** presses the "stop" button   (Page 30)
           Cut taped dialogue

Cue 10   **Bruton** switches on the music   (Page 36)
           Bring up music on stereo

Cue 11   **Bruton** switches off the music   (Page 36)
           Cut music on stereo

ACT II

Cue 12   **Neville** presses the "play" button   (Page 47)
           Taped dialogue as p. 47

Cue 13	**Neville** presses the "stop" button *Cut taped dialogue*	(Page 47)
Cue 14	**Neville** fires the rifle *Award shatters*	(Page 55)
Cue 15	**Martin** switches on the stereo *Music*	(Page 64)
Cue 16	**Bruton** switches off the music *Cut music*	(Page 69)
Cue 17	**Celia** switches on the stereo *Music*	(Page 70)

CPSIA information can be obtained at www.ICGtesting.com
Printed in the USA
LVOW10s1546080816

499499LV00001B/318/P